Verse by Verse Commentary on the Book of

SECOND
CORINTHIANS

Enduring Word Commentary Series
By David Guzik

The grass withers, the flower fades,
but the word of our God stands forever.
Isaiah 40:8

Table of Contents

For Our Daughter
Aan-Sofie Rebecka

2 Corinthians 1 - The God of All Comfort

A. Paul's trouble in Asia.

1. (1-2) Introduction.

Paul, an apostle of Jesus Christ by the will of God, and Timothy *our* brother, to the church of God which is at Corinth, with all the saints who are in all Achaia: Grace to you and peace from God our Father and the Lord Jesus Christ.

a. **Paul, an apostle of Jesus Christ**: Paul's introduction of himself as an **apostle** is both familiar and necessary because he was held in low regard among the Christians in Corinth. They had to remember and recognize his apostolic credentials.

i. **By the will of God** strengthens the point. Paul was not an apostle by the decision or desire of any man, including himself. Paul was an apostle **by the will of God**. Even if the Corinthian Christians held him in low regard, it did not diminish his standing as an **apostle** before God.

b. **With all the saints**: It is remarkable that Paul freely calls the Corinthian Christians **saints**, considering their many problems. We often use the term **saints** in a different way today, applying it to the "super-spiritual" instead of those who are simply set apart by a relationship of trust in Jesus Christ.

i. **All the saints who are in all Achaia** shows us that Paul intended his letters to be shared among the churches. They weren't just for the Christians in the city of Corinth but for all the Christians in the region who might read the letters.

c. **Grace** and **peace**: These are familiar greetings of Paul (used in all 13 of his New Testament letters), but we never get the impression that they are used insincerely.

d. **From God our Father**: This reminds us that we are children of God, yet not in the same exact sense as Jesus is the Son of God. We are sons of God, not by nature, but by election; not by ancestry but by adoption; not by right but by redemption.

2. (3-4) Praise to the God of all comfort.

Blessed *be* the God and Father of our Lord Jesus Christ, the Father of mercies and God of all comfort, who comforts us in all our tribulation, that we may be able to comfort those who are in any trouble, with the comfort with which we ourselves are comforted by God.

a. **Father of mercies and God of all comfort**: Paul opens this letter by praising the God who gives so much mercy and comfort to the apostle and all believers. We get the feeling that Paul knows the mercy and comfort of God on a first-hand basis.

i. The words **all comfort** in this passage come from the ancient Greek word *paraklesis*. The idea behind this word for **comfort** in the New Testament is always more than soothing sympathy. It has the idea of strengthening, of helping, of making strong. The idea behind this word is communicated by the Latin word for **comfort** (*fortis*), which also means "brave."

ii. "Here was a man, who never knew but what he might be dead the next day, for his enemies were many, and cruel, and mighty; and yet he spent a great part of his time in praising and blessing God." (Spurgeon)

b. **God of all comfort**: Paul considers the Father a comforter, a Paraclete (*paraklesis*). We also know that the Holy Spirit is our Paraclete (John 14:16, 14:26, 15:26, 16:7) and that God the Son is our Paraclete (1 John 2:1, Hebrews 2:18, Luke 2:25). God, in every aspect of His being, is full of comfort, strength, and help for us.

c. **That we may be able to comfort those who are in any trouble**: One great purpose of God in comforting us is to enable us to bring comfort to others. God's comfort can be given and received through others.

i. Often, we never receive the comfort God wants to give us through another person. Pride keeps us from revealing our needs to others, so we never receive the comfort God would give us through them.

ii. "Even *spiritual* comforts are not given us for our use alone; they, like all the gifts of God, are given that they may be distributed, or become instruments of help to others. A minister's trials and comforts are permitted and sent for the benefit of the Church. What a miserable preacher must he be who has all his divinity by study and learning, and nothing by experience!" (Clarke)

iii. "Mr. Knox, a little before his death, rose out of his bed; and being asked wherefore, being so sick, he would offer to rise? He answered, that he had had sweet meditations of the resurrection of Jesus Christ that night, and now he would go into the pulpit, and impart to others the comforts that he felt in his soul." (Trapp)

3. (5-7) Paul's personal suffering and consolation.

For as the sufferings of Christ abound in us, so our consolation also abounds through Christ. Now if we are afflicted, *it is* **for your consolation and salvation, which is effective for enduring the same sufferings which we also suffer. Or if we are comforted,** *it is* **for your consolation and salvation. And our hope for you** *is* **steadfast, because we know that as you are partakers of the sufferings, so also** *you will partake* **of the consolation.**

a. **The sufferings of Christ abound in us**: Paul had a life filled with suffering. He describes some of these sufferings in 2 Corinthians 11:23-28: *stripes . . . prisons . . . beatings . . . stonings . . . shipwrecked . . . perils of waters . . . robbers . . . in perils of my own countrymen, in perils of the Gentiles, in perils in the city, in perils in the wilderness, in perils in the sea, in perils among false brethren; in weariness and toil, in sleeplessness often, in hunger and thirst, in fastings often, in cold and nakedness.* Yet, Paul knew that all his sufferings were really **the sufferings of Christ**.

b. **So our consolation also abounds through Christ**: Because Paul's sufferings were **the sufferings of Christ**, Jesus was not distant from Paul in his trials. He was right there, identifying with the apostle and comforting him.

i. "As the hotter the day, the greater the dew at night; so the hotter the time of trouble, the greater the dews of refreshing from God." (Trapp)

ii. We can count on it: when sufferings **abound, consolation also abounds**. Jesus is there to bring comfort if we will receive it. Of course, this assumes we are not suffering *as a murderer, a thief, an evildoer, or as a busybody in other people's matters. Yet if anyone suffers as a Christian, let him not be ashamed, but let him glorify God in this matter.* (1 Peter 4:15-16)

iii. "It is not of suffering as suffering that the apostle here speaks. There is no tendency in pain to produce holiness. It is only of Christian suffering and of that sufferings of Christians, that is, of suffering endured for Christ and in a Christian manner, that the apostle says it is connected with salvation, or that it tends to work out for those who suffer an eternal weight of glory." (Hodge)

c. **Our consolation also abounds through Christ**. God may allow situations in our life where our only **consolation** is found **through Christ**. Sometimes we think the only consolation is found in a change of circumstances, but God wants to console us right in the midst of our difficult circumstances, and to do it **through Christ**.

i. This is the same idea Jesus expressed in John 16:33: *In the world you will have tribulation; but be of good cheer, I have overcome the world.*

ii. Jesus also suffered, therefore He is fully qualified to comfort us in our time of trial. (Hebrews 2:18)

d. **If we are afflicted, it is for your consolation and salvation**: If Paul and other ministers were afflicted, it was for the sake of God's people (like the Corinthian Christians). God had a larger purpose in Paul's suffering than just working on Paul himself. God brought **consolation and salvation** to others through Paul's sufferings.

i. How could God bring **consolation and salvation** to others through Paul's suffering? As suffering brought Paul closer to God and made him rely more and more on God alone, Paul was a more effective minister. He was more usable in the hand of God to bring **consolation and salvation** to God's people.

ii. Whenever we pray, "Lord, just use me. I just want to be used by You to touch the lives of others," we do not realize that we pray a dangerous prayer. Through this good prayer, we invite God to bring suffering into our lives if that is the proper tool to make us more able to bring **consolation and salvation** to the lives of others.

e. **Which is effective for enduring the same sufferings which we also suffer**: The consolation and salvation the Corinthian Christians received from Paul's suffering were at work in the Corinthians, making them able to endure **the same sufferings** Paul and the other apostles endured.

i. Significantly, Paul writes of **the same sufferings**. It is unlikely the Corinthian Christians were suffering in exactly the same way Paul was. Probably, not one of them could match the list Paul made in 2 Corinthians 11:23-28. Yet, Paul can say they are **the same sufferings** because he recognizes that the exact circumstances of suffering are not as important as what God does and wants to do through the suffering. Christians should never get into a "competition" of comparing suffering. There is a sense in which we all share **the same sufferings**.

ii. Of course, sometimes it is useful to compare our sufferings to those of others - to see how *light* our burden really is! It is easy for us to think our small problems are really much larger than they are.

iii. The New Testament idea of suffering is broad and not easily limited to just one kind of trouble (like persecution). The ancient Greek word for suffering (*thlipsis*) originally had the idea of actual physical pressure. In old England, heavy weights were put on certain condemned criminals until they were "pressed to death." *Thlipsis* describes that kind of "pressing."

f. **Effective for enduring**: God's desire is that we would be **enduring** through suffering. The ancient Greek word for **enduring** is *hupomone*. It isn't the idea of passive, bleak acceptance, but of the kind of spirit that can triumph over pain and suffering to achieve the goal. It is the spirit of the marathon runner, not of the victim in the dentist's chair.

g. **Or, if we are comforted, it is for your consolation and salvation**: God did not work only through the *suffering* Paul endured. God also worked good things in others through the *comfort* Paul received from the Lord.

i. We see Paul living in the footsteps of Jesus, who was truly an *others-centered person*. Paul's life is not focused on himself, but on the Lord and on those whom the Lord has given him to serve. Is Paul suffering? It is so that God can do something good in the Corinthian Christians. Is Paul comforted? It is so that God can bless the Corinthian Christians. Suffering or comforted, it wasn't all about Paul; it was all about others.

ii. "We are not brought to real submission until we have been laid low by the crushing hand of God." (Calvin)

h. **We know that as you are partakers of the sufferings, so also you will partake of the consolation**: According to many passages in the New Testament, suffering is promised in the Christian life (Acts 14:22, 1 Thessalonians 3:3, Philippians 1:29, Romans 5:3). Nevertheless, we are also promised consolation in the midst of suffering.

4. (8-11) Paul's desperate trouble.

For we do not want you to be ignorant, brethren, of our trouble which came to us in Asia: that we were burdened beyond measure, above strength, so that we despaired even of life. Yes, we had the sentence of death in ourselves, that we should not trust in ourselves but in God who raises the dead, who delivered us from so great a death, and does deliver us; in whom we trust that He will still deliver *us*, you also helping together in prayer for us, that thanks may be given by many persons on our behalf for the gift *granted* to us through many.

a. **Our trouble which came to us in Asia**: We don't know the exact nature of this trouble. It was probably some type of persecution or a physical affliction made worse by Paul's missionary work.

i. There are at least five suggestions for this **trouble**:

- Fighting with "wild beasts" in Ephesus (1 Corinthians 15:32)

- Suffering 39 stripes after being brought before a Jewish court (2 Corinthians 11:24)

- The riot at Ephesus (Acts 19:23-41)

- A particular persecution shortly before Paul left for Troas (Acts 20:19 and 1 Corinthians 16:9)

- A recurring physical malady

b. **We were burdened beyond measure, above strength, so that we despaired even of life**: Whatever the problem was, it was bad. Because of this problem, Paul lived with the awareness that he might die at any time (**we had the sentence of death . . . who delivered us from so great a death**).

i. Because of the threat of death, many feel Paul's problem must have been persecution. However, the idea of a recurring physical malady isn't a bad choice. In that day, Jews could refer to sickness as "death" and healing as a "return to life." The use of the present tense in 2 Corinthians 1:4-6 and 1:9-10 imply that the problem was still with Paul as he wrote the letter. This makes it more likely - though by no means certain - that the trouble was a stubborn illness.

ii. **In ourselves** tells us that Paul's **sentence of death** was something he felt within, not something that a court of law had imposed on him from without.

c. **That we should not trust in ourselves but in God who raises the dead**: Even though the resurrection is a future event, there is a sense in which the reality and power of the resurrection touches every day for the suffering Christian. As we know by *the power of His resurrection* we will also be blessed by *the fellowship of His sufferings*. (Philippians 3:10)

d. **Who delivered us . . . and does deliver us . . . we trust that He will still deliver us**: Paul knew that God's work in our lives happens in three different verb tenses. God works in us past, present, and future.

e. **You also helping together in prayer for us**: Paul knew the value of intercessory prayer and was not shy about asking the Corinthians, despite their many spiritual problems, to pray for him. The Corinthian Christians were really **helping together** with Paul when they prayed for him.

i. Paul knew that blessing in ministry was **granted to us through many**: that is, through the prayers of **many** people. We often think of the great things God did through Paul, and we rightly admire him as a man of God. Do we think of all the people who prayed for him? Paul credited those praying people with much of his effectiveness in ministry.

ii. "Even an *apostle* felt the prayers of the Church necessary for his comfort and support. What innumerable blessings do the prayers of the followers of God draw down on those who are the objects of them!" (Clarke)

f. **Persons** is literally "faces." The idea "is that of faces upturned in prayer, the early Christian (and Jewish) attitude of prayer being one of standing with uplifted eyes and outstretched arms." (Bernard)

B. Paul defends his ministry.

1. (12-14) Paul's boast: his integrity and simplicity in ministry towards the Corinthian Christians.

For our boasting is this: the testimony of our conscience that we conducted ourselves in the world in simplicity and godly sincerity, not with fleshly wisdom but by the grace of God, and more abundantly toward you. For we are not writing any other things to you than what you read or understand. Now I trust you will understand, even to the end (as also you have understood us in part), that we are your boast as you also *are* ours, in the day of the Lord Jesus.

a. **The testimony of our conscience**: In this section, Paul defends himself against the accusation that he is fickle and unreliable. Here, he simply states that he has a clear conscience before God and trusts that the Corinthian Christians will understand this.

b. **We conducted ourselves in the world in simplicity and godly sincerity, not with fleshly wisdom**: The Corinthian Christians were so accustomed to dealing with ministers who were calculating and manipulative, they figured Paul must be the same way. Therefore, when Paul said he was coming to them (1 Corinthians 16:5) but did not, they figured he was just manipulating them. Paul lets them know this was not the case.

i. The Corinthian Christians had become *cynical*. They believed that everyone had bad motives and was out for personal gain and power. They didn't trust Paul because they were cynical.

c. **We are not writing any other things to you than what you read or understand**: Paul wanted the Corinthian Christians to know he had no "hidden meanings" in his letters. His meaning was right out on top for all to see.

i. A cynical heart always thinks, "You say *this*, but you really mean *that*. You aren't telling the truth." Paul assured the Corinthian Christians that he really told the truth and he didn't communicate with manipulative hidden meanings.

ii. "In Paul's life there were no hidden actions, no hidden motives and no hidden meanings." (Barclay)

2. (15-17) Paul considers the accusation that he is unreliable and can't be trusted.

And in this confidence I intended to come to you before, that you might have a second benefit; to pass by way of you to Macedonia, to come again from Macedonia to you, and be helped by you on my way to Judea. Therefore, when I was planning this, did I do it lightly? Or the things I plan, do I plan according to the flesh, that with me there should be Yes, Yes, and No, No?

a. **I intended to come to you before**: The Corinthian Christians accused Paul of being unreliable and untrustworthy because he said he would come at a certain time and did not. He was unable to come as planned, so instead he sent a letter.

i. In 1 Corinthians 16:5-7 Paul promised to see the Corinthians after his trip through Macedonia.

ii. He changed his plans and decided to see them first on his way to Macedonia and then again on his way back, to give them **a second benefit** (2 Corinthians 1:15-16).

iii. Paul made the first visit on the way to Macedonia, but it was painful for both him and the Corinthians because it was full of confrontation (*I would not come again to you in sorrow*, 2 Corinthians 2:1).

iv. At some time after this visit, Paul (or perhaps his representative) was openly insulted in Corinth by someone from the "anti-Paul" party (2 Corinthians 2:5-10, 7:12).

v. Because the first visit was so unpleasant and sensing no benefit in a second visit, Paul abandoned his plan to see them on the way back from Macedonia.

vi. Titus was sent from Ephesus to Corinth with the "severe letter" (2 Corinthians 2:3-9). Titus was also there to collect the contribution for the church in Judea, but the Corinthians didn't give as they should have.

vii. Paul left Ephesus and suffered his "affliction in Asia."

viii. Paul then went to Macedonia and among other things, he organized a collection for the needy Christians in Judea. Titus met Paul in Macedonia, and told Paul about the Corinthians' response to the "severe letter."

ix. Later from Macedonia, Paul wrote 2 Corinthians when he heard of more problems at Corinth. The letter was probably written in the fall of 56 A.D.

b. **Helped by you on my way**: This acknowledges the ancient custom of sending a traveler on his way at the outset of his journey. In the ancient world, when a distinguished guest came to a city, his friends and supporters met him a distance away from the city and walked into the city with him. They also sent him away the same way, walking with him for some distance away from the city.

c. **When I was planning this, did I do it lightly?** The Corinthian Christians accused Paul of being fickle and insisted that if Paul were a man of integrity he would have come in person. Paul's change in plans made the Corinthian Christians say that Paul must be a man who says **Yes** but means **No** and says **No** but means **Yes**.

i. Paul was criticized as a man who couldn't decide on a plan or who could not carry through on a plan. His enemies among the Christians in Corinth seized on these circumstances to make Paul look bad.

ii. It was all right for the Corinthian Christians to be disappointed that Paul didn't come and visit them. But they were wrong in trying to *blame* Paul for the disappointment. They needed to see Paul's heart and God's hand in the circumstances.

3. (18) Paul denies the accusation made against him.

But *as* God *is* faithful, our word to you was not Yes and No.

a. **As God is faithful**: Paul can say, "**As God is faithful**, so we were faithful in what we said to you." Paul was such a man of integrity that he could liken his truthfulness to God's faithfulness.

i. "*As God is true* to his promises, so he hath taught me to be true to mine." (Poole)

b. **Our word to you was not Yes and No**: Paul did not say **Yes** and mean **No** or say **No** and mean **Yes**, as the Corinthian Christians accused him.

4. (19-22) Paul knew their accusations were wrong based on spiritual reasons.

For the Son of God, Jesus Christ, who was preached among you by us; by me, Silvanus, and Timothy, was not Yes and No, but in Him was Yes. For all the promises of God in Him *are* Yes, and in Him Amen, to the glory of God through us. Now He who establishes us with you in Christ and has anointed us *is* God, who also has sealed us and given us the Spirit in our hearts as a guarantee.

a. **Jesus Christ, who was preached among you by us . . . was not Yes and No**: Paul preached a Jesus who is completely reliable and worthy of trust. It wasn't right for the apostle of such a faithful Savior to be so quickly considered unreliable and untrustworthy.

i. Paul alludes to an important principle: The message affects the messenger. Paul could not so sincerely and so strongly preach a Jesus who is **not Yes and No** and be untouched by that Jesus. Understanding this should have made the Corinthian Christians more trusting towards Paul.

b. **For all the promises of God in Him are Yes and in Him Amen**: Can we imagine God the Father ever saying "no" to God the Son? God the Father will always say **Yes** to the Son and will always affirm what the Son says (**Amen**).

i. "We might never have had this precious verse if Paul had not been so ill-treated by these men of Corinth. They did him great wrong, and caused him much sorrow of heart . . . yet you see how the evil was overruled by God for good, and through their unsavoury gossip and slander this sweet sentence was pressed out of Paul." (Spurgeon)

c. **He who establishes us . . . and has anointed us is God, who also has sealed us and given us the Spirit**: Paul and his associates were commissioned by God and filled with the Holy Spirit. Understanding this should have made the Corinthian Christians reject hasty and unfounded accusations against Paul.

d. **Anointed us . . . sealed us . . . a guarantee**: Paul refers to three aspects of the Holy Spirit's work within us.

i. **Has anointed us**: The only other place where the New Testament speaks about *anointing* is in 1 John 2:20 and 2:27. Every use speaks of an anointing that is common to all believers, not a special anointing for a few Christian superstars. The idea behind **anointed** is that we are prepared and empowered for service. The fact that we are **anointed** means that we share something with the Old Testament prophets, priests, and kings who were also **anointed** ones.

ii. **Sealed us**: In the ancient world, a seal was used to *identify* and to *protect*. If something was **sealed**, everyone knew who it belonged to (the seal had an insignia), and the seal prevented anyone else from tampering with the item. The Holy Spirit is upon us to *identify* us and to *protect* us.

iii. **A guarantee**: The word **guarantee** is the word for a down payment. We have been given the Holy Spirit as a down payment for the fullness of what God will do. The Holy Spirit is a pledge of greater things to come. As Christians, God has purchased us on the lay-away plan and has given us an impressive down payment. He won't walk away from the final payment because He has so much invested already.

5. (23-24) Paul knew their accusations were wrong based on his own personal reasons.

Moreover I call God as witness against my soul, that to spare you I came no more to Corinth. Not that we have dominion over your faith, but are fellow workers for your joy; for by faith you stand.

a. **I call God as witness against my soul**: Paul is taking a serious oath. While Jesus said we should live our lives in such a way so that oaths are not necessary (Matthew 5:33-37), it does not mean that oaths are prohibited. On occasion, even God swears an oath (Hebrews 6:13).

b. **That to spare you I came no more to Corinth**: The Corinthian Christians had assumed that Paul did not come in person because of selfish reasons. They wanted to think he simply was not a man of integrity or was just afraid of conflict. Paul sets them straight: **to spare you I came no more**. Paul insists that it was out of concern for the Corinthian Christians that he did not make the visit at that particular time.

c. **Not that we have dominion over your faith**: Paul is careful to point out that he is no one's lord in the church, even though he is an apostle.

i. It has been said that God reserves three things to Himself:

- First, to make something of nothing
- Second, to know future events
- Third, to have dominion over men's consciences

ii. Sadly, there are far too many that are entirely willing to take dominion over other believers in a manner that Paul would not. "The SACRED WRITINGS, and they *alone*, contain what is necessary to faith and practice; and that no man, number of men, society, church, council, presbytery, consistory, or conclave, has *dominion over any man's faith*. The word of God alone is his rule, and to its Author he is to give account of the use he has made of it." (Clarke)

d. **Fellow workers for your joy**: Instead of seeing himself as some kind of "lord" over the Corinthian Christians, Paul gives a great description of what ministers should be: **fellow workers**. Leaders among Christians should work alongside their people to increase their **joy**.

2 Corinthians 2 - The Strategy of Satan and the Victory of Jesus

A. Paul's change of plans: more reasons why the Corinthians misinterpreted why he did not come to them a second time.

1. (1-2) Paul remembers his sorrowful visit to the Corinthians.

But I determined this within myself, that I would not come again to you in sorrow. For if I make you sorrowful, then who is he who makes me glad but the one who is made sorrowful by me?

a. **But I determined**: Carrying on the thought from chapter one, Paul defends himself against the Corinthian Christians. Some among them criticized him because he changed his travel plans and did not come when he planned to. They used this change of plans to say of Paul, "He is unreliable and untrustworthy. We don't need to listen to him at all." But Paul explains there were many reasons why he did not come as planned, one of them being he was trying to *spare* the Corinthians (2 Corinthians 1:23).

b. **I would not come again to you in sorrow**: Paul's most recent visit to Corinth was full of conflict and unpleasantness. So he **determined** that he would not have another "sorrowful" visit with the Corinthians.

i. "Because of the scandals that were among them he could not see them comfortably; and therefore he determined not to see them at all till he had reason to believe that those evils were put away." (Clarke)

c. **If I make you sorrowful, then who is he who makes me glad**? Paul also knew that another painful visit would not be good for him. The constant conflict with the Corinthian Christians could really damage his relationship with them.

i. It seems that Paul thought it best to give the Corinthian Christians a little room, and give them space to repent and get their act together. He didn't want to rebuke and admonish them all the time. Since this was Paul's heart, he knew that another visit of the same kind would be of little benefit for either Paul or the Corinthian Christians.

2. (3-4) Instead of a second visit, Paul wrote a letter.

And I wrote this very thing to you, lest, when I came, I should have sorrow over those from whom I ought to have joy, having confidence in you all that my joy is *the joy* of you all. For out of much affliction and anguish of heart I wrote to you, with many tears, not that you should be grieved, but that you might know the love which I have so abundantly for you.

a. **And I wrote this very thing to you**: Paul wisely understood that considering all the circumstances, a letter was better than a personal visit. A letter could show Paul's heart, yet not give as much opportunity for the deterioration of their relationship. It would give them room to repent and get right with God and Paul again.

i. Where is this letter that Paul mentions? Some good scholars see the "sorrowful letter" as 1 Corinthians, but it seems better to think of it as another letter that we don't have. Does this mean that something is missing from our Bibles? Not at all. Not every letter that Paul wrote was inspired Scripture for all God's people in all ages. We can trust that what Paul wrote in the missing letter was perfect for the Corinthian Christians at that time, but not perfect for us; otherwise, God would have preserved it. We shouldn't think that everything Paul or the other Bible writers wrote was necessarily Scripture.

b. **Lest when I came, I should have sorrow**: Paul hoped that his letter would get all the painful work out of the way. Then when he did visit them personally, it would be a pleasant visit because they would have taken advantage of the opportunity he gave them to get right.

c. **Over those from whom I ought to have joy**: The bad conduct of the Corinthian Christians was all the more troubling considering how they *should* have treated the apostle who gave them so much.

i. "All evils, as elements, are most troublesome, when out of their proper place, as impiety in professors; injustice in judges; unkindness or untowardness in a people toward their pastor." (Trapp)

d. **Out of much affliction and anguish of heart I wrote to you**: Paul did not enjoy confronting the Corinthian Christians. It was hard for him to do, and he did it **with many tears**. His goal was **not that you should be grieved**, but instead that the Corinthian Christians would know **the love which I have so abundantly for you.**

i. It would take some maturity for the Corinthian Christians to receive Paul's correction this way. It is easy for us to think a person offering correction is our enemy and sometimes is against us. But usually others bring correction because they love us, as Paul loved the Corinthian Christians. His goal was not to grieve them, but to love them.

ii. "Where I have known that there existed a measure of disaffection to myself, I have not recognised it, unless it has been forced upon me, but have, on the contrary, acted towards the opposing person with all the more courtesy and friendliness, and I have never heard any more of the matter. If I had treated the good man as an opponent, he would have done his best to take the part assigned him, and carry it out to his own credit." (Spurgeon)

e. **I wrote to you, with many tears**: "St. Paul's Epistles were written rather with tears than with ink." (Trapp)

B. Paul's appeal to forgive the brother who had sinned.

1. (5-7) Paul recommends that the Corinthian Christians forgive the brother who had sinned (and repented) among them.

But if anyone has caused grief, he has not grieved me, but all of you to some extent; not to be too severe. This punishment which *was inflicted* by the majority *is* sufficient for such a man, so that, on the contrary, you *ought* rather to forgive and comfort *him*, lest perhaps such a one be swallowed up with too much sorrow.

a. **If anyone has caused grief**: Paul displays real pastoral wisdom and compassion. He refers to a specific person among the Corinthians, but he does not name the man. Certainly, this man is happy his name was not recorded in God's eternal word.

b. Who is this man? He is probably the same one that Paul told the Corinthian Christians to confront in 1 Corinthians 5. The phrase **such a man** is used in both books to describe the man sinning in an incestuous affair. He lived immorally with his stepmother.

i. Some commentators disagree and think Paul speaks of another man all together. They believe this man sinned by insulting Paul to his face during his "painful visit." But 2 Corinthians 2:10 says that Paul expected the Corinthian Christians to forgive the brother *first*, then *he* would forgive. If the offense had been something personal towards Paul, we would expect it to be the other way around. In fact, Paul plainly says **he has not grieved me**. His first offense was not against Paul. So, it is likely that **such a man** was the one Paul said must be confronted in 1 Corinthians 5.

c. **Not to be too severe**: Apparently, the man was put under the church's discipline, even as Paul instructed in 1 Corinthians 5. He received **this punishment which was inflicted by the majority**. After receiving the punishment, the man apparently repented, but the Corinthian Christians would not receive him back! Therefore, Paul tells them to not **be too severe**, to consider their punishment **sufficient**, and to **forgive and comfort** the man.

> i. In 1 Corinthians 5, Paul sharply rebuked the Corinthian Christians for their casual attitude towards this man and his sin. He commanded them *when you are gathered together . . . deliver such a one to Satan for the destruction of his flesh* (1 Corinthians 5:4-5). Paul told them to put the man outside the spiritual and social protection of the church family until he repented.

> ii. It worked! The Corinthian Christians applied the **punishment**, and apparently the man repented. Now, Paul must tell the Corinthian Christians to restore the repentant man.

d. **Forgive and comfort him**: They were just as wrong in withholding forgiveness and restoration to the man when he repented as they were to welcome him with open, approving arms when he was in sin. The Corinthian Christians found it easy to err on either extreme, either being too lenient or too harsh.

> i. Paul told them to do more than **forgive**; he also told them to **comfort**. "There may be a judicial forgiveness which is hard, and leaves the soul always conscious of the past. Comfort takes the soul to heart, and forgets. That is how God forgives, and so should we who are His children." (Morgan)

> ii. "If discipline is largely lacking in the Church of today, so also is the grace of forgiving and comforting those who, having done wrong, are truly repentant. How often, alas! souls have been indeed swallowed up with overmuch sorrow because of the harshness and suspicion of Christian people toward them in view of some wrong which they have done . . . Love never slights holiness; but holiness never slays love." (Morgan)

e. **Lest perhaps such a one be swallowed up with too much sorrow**: Their harsh stance towards this man had a real danger: By withholding restoration and forgiveness from the man they risked ruining him, causing him to be **swallowed up with too much sorrow**.

> i. "It is a saying of Austin, Let a man grieve for his sin, and then joy for his grief. Sorrow for sin, if it so far exceed, as that thereby we are disabled for the discharge of our duties, it is a sinful sorrow, yea, though it be for sin." (Trapp)

ii. *Restoring* work towards sinners is just as important as *rebuking* work. Trapp cites an extreme example of the failure to restore: "The Papists burnt some that recanted at the stake, saying, that they would send them out of the world while they were in a good mind."

2. (8-11) Understanding Satan's strategy in the matter.

Therefore I urge you to reaffirm *your* love to him. For to this end I also wrote, that I might put you to the test, whether you are obedient in all things. Now whom you forgive anything, I also *forgive*. For if indeed I have forgiven anything, I have forgiven that one for your sakes in the presence of Christ, lest Satan should take advantage of us; for we are not ignorant of his devices.

a. **Therefore I urge you to reaffirm your love to him**: Since the man responded to the correction and repented, it was time for love and healing. They needed to **reaffirm** their **love to him**.

i. "When the offender is made to feel that, while his sin is punished, he himself is loved; and that the end aimed at is not his suffering but his good, he is more likely to be brought to repentance." (Hodge)

b. **That I might put you to the test**: Paul wrote strongly in 1 Corinthians 5, and the Corinthian Christians met the test by doing what Paul said to do. Now he puts them **to the test** again, telling them to show love to the repentant brother.

i. Paul wanted the Corinthian Christians to be **obedient in all things**. Would they find it easier to be obedient when he asked them to be "tough" than when he asked them to show love and restoration?

c. **I forgive also**: The offending man had also sinned against Paul in some way, either directly or indirectly. Paul expected the Corinthian Christians to take the lead in showing the man forgiveness and restoration.

i. Even if the church must treat someone as an unbeliever as a matter of church discipline, we must remember how we are to treat unbelievers: with love and concern, hoping to win them to Jesus, anxious for repentance.

ii. There is no inconsistency: If your brother sins, rebuke him. If he repents, forgive him. (Luke 17:3)

d. **Lest Satan should take advantage of us**: Paul knew this was of special concern because Satan looks to **take advantage** of our mistakes, as a church and as individuals.

i. Trapp describes how **Satan** loves to **take advantage**: "That wily merchant, that greedy blood-sucker, that devoureth not widows' houses, but most men's souls."

ii. **Take advantage** (the ancient Greek word *pleonekteo*) is used in four other verses in the New Testament (2 Corinthians 7:2, 12:17-18, and 1 Thessalonians 4:6). It has the idea of cheating someone out of something that belongs to them. When we are ignorant of Satan's strategies, he is able to take things from us that belong to us in Jesus, things like peace, joy, fellowship, a sense of forgiveness, and victory.

e. **For we are not ignorant of his devices**: Their failure to show love to the repentant man could be used as a strategy of Satan.

i. To withhold forgiveness from the repentant is to play into the hands of Satan. "There is nothing more dangerous than to give Satan a chance of reducing a sinner to despair. Whenever we fail to comfort those that are moved to a sincere confession of their sin, we play into Satan's hands." (Calvin)

f. **His devices**: Satan has specific **devices** (strategies) he uses against us to **take advantage of us**. Paul could say that he was **not ignorant** of Satan's strategies, but many Christians cannot say the same thing.

i. Satan's strategy *against the sinning man* was first focused on lust, then he used hopelessness and despair. Satan's strategy *against the church* was first the toleration of evil, then using undue severity in punishment. Satan's strategy *against Paul* was to simply make him so stressed and upset over the Corinthian Christians that he lost peace and was less effective in ministry.

ii. Calvin defined these **devices** as "the artful schemes and tricks of which believers ought to be aware, and will be if they allow the Spirit of God to rule in them." Are you allowing the Spirit to make you aware of Satan's strategy against you right now? What weak point is he trying to exploit? Where is Satan trying to get a foothold into your life? Are you **ignorant of his devices**?

C. The triumph of Jesus Christ.

1. (12-13) What Paul did on his way to Macedonia.

Furthermore, when I came to Troas to *preach* Christ's gospel, and a door was opened to me by the Lord. I had no rest in my spirit, because I did not find Titus my brother; but taking my leave of them, I departed for Macedonia.

a. **A door was opened to me by the Lord**: Paul was interested in ministering where God opened doors. The only way our work for God will be blessed is when it is *directed service*.

i. Where we see **a door . . . opened**, we can have faith that God will bless the ministry. "Where the master sets up a light, there is some work to be done; where he sends forth his labourers, there is some harvest to be gotten in." (Trapp)

b. **I had no rest in my spirit, because I did not find Titus my brother:** Even though there was an open door, Paul felt he could not do all that he needed to if he did not have **Titus** there. Paul did not regard himself as a one-man show; he knew he needed other people with him and beside him.

In 2 Corinthians 2:13, Paul mentions his departure for Macedonia. In 2 Corinthians 7:5, he writes about his arrival in Macedonia. In between - from 2 Corinthians 2:14 through 7:4 - is sometimes called "the great digression." In this extended section, Paul describes and defends his ministry as an apostle.

2. (14) Jesus, the triumphant leader.

Now thanks *be* to God who always leads us in triumph in Christ, and through us diffuses the fragrance of His knowledge in every place.

a. **Thanks be to God who always leads us**: Paul dealt with criticism from the Corinthian Christians, who said he was unreliable and fickle because of his travel plans. He has explained himself and his reasons for not arriving when he had previously planned. More than anything, he wanted the Corinthian Christians to know he is following Jesus Christ as his General. More than any plan he may declare to the Corinthian Christians, Paul's plan is to follow Jesus Christ.

b. **Who always leads us in triumph in Christ**: Here, Paul takes an image from the Roman world, seeing Jesus as the victorious, conquering general in a triumphal parade. A Roman triumphal parade was given to successful generals as they returned from their conquests.

i. "The idea is borrowed from an ancient Roman triumph, which to the eyes of the world of that day was the most glorious spectacle which the imagination could conceive." (Meyer)

ii. "In a Triumph the procession of the victorious general marched through the streets of Rome to the Capitol . . . First came the state officials and the senate. Then came the trumpeters. Then were carried the spoils taken from the conquered land . . . Then came the pictures of the conquered land and models of conquered citadels and ships. There followed the white bull for sacrifice which would be made. Then there walked the captive princes, leaders and generals in chains, shortly to be flung into prison and in all probability almost immediately to be executed. Then came the lictors bearing their rods, followed by the musicians with their lyres; then the priests swinging their censers with the sweet-smelling incense burning in them. After that came the general himself . . . finally came the army wearing all their decorations and shouting *Io triumphe!* Their cry of triumph. As the procession moved through the streets, all decorated and garlanded, amid the cheering crowds, it made a tremendous day which might happen only once in a lifetime." (Barclay)

iii. "That is the picture that is in Paul's mind. He sees Christ marching in triumph throughout the world, and himself in that conquering train. It is a triumph which, Paul is certain, nothing can stop." (Barclay) And, Paul sees himself as sharing in the triumph of Jesus, the Captain of the Lord's Army, and Paul is one of the Lord's chief officers!

c. **Leads us**: Paul wanted the Corinthian Christians to realize that he followed his general, Jesus Christ. Paul can almost see Jesus' triumphal parade winding its way through the whole Roman Empire, throughout the entire world.

d. **Diffuses the fragrance of His knowledge**: Fragrance, in the form of incense, was common at the Roman triumphal parade. In Paul's mind, this **fragrance** is like the **knowledge** of God, which people can smell as the triumphal parade comes by.

i. No sense remains in the memory like scent. There is nothing we remember more strongly than pleasant smells, except perhaps unpleasant smells. "Thus the apostle wished that his life might be a sweet perfume, floating on the air, reminding me, and above all reminding God, of Christ." (Meyer)

ii. "A sweet savour of Christ! It does not consist so much in what we do, but in our manner of doing it; not so much in our words or deeds, as in an indefinable sweetness, tenderness, courtesy, unselfishness, and desire to please others to their edification. It is the breath and fragrance of a life hidden with Christ in God, and deriving its aroma from fellowship with Him. Wrap the habits of your soul in the sweet lavender of your Lord's character." (Meyer)

2. (15-16a) The triumphal parade means different things to different people.

For we are to God the fragrance of Christ among those who are being saved and among those who are perishing. To the one *we are* the aroma of death *leading* to death, and to the other the aroma of life *leading* to life.

a. **To the one we are the aroma of death leading to death, and to the other the aroma of life leading to life**: The scent of incense burnt to the gods in a Roman triumphal parade smelled wonderful to a Roman. The same aroma was a bad smell to a captive prisoner of war in the parade, who would soon be executed or sold into slavery.

b. We are to God the fragrance of Christ among those who are being saved and among those who are perishing: In the same way, the message of the gospel is a message of life to some and a message of condemnation to those who reject it (John 3:17-21).

> i. "The same happens to the present day to those who receive and to those who reject the Gospel: it is the *means* of *salvation* to the former, it is the means of *destruction* to the latter; for they are not only *not saved* because they do not believe the Gospel, but they are *condemned* because they *reject* it." (Clarke)

3. (16b-17) Paul briefly characterizes his ministry.

And who *is* sufficient for these things? For we are not, as so many, peddling the word of God; but as of sincerity, but as from God, we speak in the sight of God in Christ.

a. Who is sufficient for these things? When Paul thinks of the greatness of God's plan, he wonders if anyone **is sufficient** to play a role in it. "In himself, no one is. But some one has to preach Christ and Paul proceeds to show that he is sufficient." (Robertson)

> i. "This is a great work, first to consult the mind and will of God, and find it out by study and meditation; then faithfully to communicate it unto people, without any vain or corrupt mixtures (which do but adulterate the word preached); then to apply it to the consciences of those that hear us. *Who is sufficient for these things?* That is, to discharge the office of the ministry in the preaching of the gospel, as men ought to preach it." (Poole)

b. For we are not, as so many, peddling the word of God: The word **peddling** has the idea of "adulterating" or "watering down" for gain, and was especially used of a wine seller who watered down the wine for bigger profits. Paul was not like others who watered down the gospel for gain.

> i. Trapp on **peddling the word of God**: "This is one of the 'devil's depths,' Revelation 2:24; whereunto God's faithful ministers are perfect strangers."

c. As of sincerity: **Sincerity** is the ancient Greek word *eilikrineia*, which means "pure" or "transparent." Barclay says, "It may describe something which can bear the test of being held up to the light of the sun and looked at with the sun shining through it." Paul's message and ministry did not have hidden motives or agendas.

d. We speak in the sight of God in Christ: Paul was always aware that his first audience in ministry was God Himself. Every word he spoke, he spoke **in the sight of God**.

2 Corinthians 3 - The Glory of the New Covenant

A. Paul's letter of recommendation.

1. (1-2) Does Paul need a letter of recommendation? He has one - the Corinthian Christians themselves.

Do we begin again to commend ourselves? Or do we need, as some *others*, epistles of commendation to you or *letters* of commendation from you? You are our epistle written in our hearts, known and read by all men.

a. **Epistles of commendation**: Such letters were common and necessary in the early church. A false prophet or apostle could travel from city to city and easily say, "Paul sent me, so you should support me." To help guard against problems like this, letters of recommendation were often sent with Christians as they traveled.

i. Paul himself sent **letters of commendation** on many occasions (Romans 16:1-2, 1 Corinthians 16:3, 16:10-11, 2 Corinthians 8:16-24). Now Paul will describe *his* letter of recommendation.

b. **You are our epistle**: Paul has a letter of recommendation, but it isn't written on paper. Paul says the letter is **written in our hearts**, and it is **known and read by all men**.

i. There was nothing wrong with a letter of commendation written on paper, but how much better to have a *living* letter of commendation! The Christians at Corinth, along with groups of Christians wherever Paul had worked, were Paul's "living letter" to validate his ministry.

ii. The best analogy in today's world might be a certificate of ordination. Many people think that a certificate of ordination means that you have the credentials of ministry. While there is an important purpose in a public ordination to ministry, a piece of paper in itself never is a proper credential. The true credentials of the ministry are changed lives, living epistles. We might almost say, keep your paper to yourself and show us the changed lives from your ministry.

iii. "Nothing so commends a minister as the proficiency of his people." (Poole) "The fruitfulness of the people is the preacher's testimonial." (Trapp)

iv. Many think the main reason God granted the miraculous signs and wonders among the apostles in the Book of Acts to serve as a "letter of commendation" to their apostolic ministry. If this was the case, it makes sense that the miraculous gifts of the Spirit would cease when the apostles passed from the scene, because there would no longer be an apostolic ministry to authenticate. However, it is significant that Paul does *not* say, "miracles are our epistle of commendation." Paul apparently did not believe his primary "letter of recommendation" was found in miraculous signs but found in miraculously changed lives.

2. (3) The writing of Paul's letter of recommendation.

Clearly *you are* an epistle of Christ, ministered by us, written not with ink but by the Spirit of the living God, not on tablets of stone but on tablets of flesh, *that is*, of the heart.

a. **An epistle of Christ**: Paul's letter of recommendation has an author, Jesus Christ. The Corinthian Christians were indeed Paul's letter of recommendation, yet he realized that he did not write that letter - Jesus did. Paul is not trying to say, "I made you the Christians you are," but he is saying, "God used me to make you the Christians you are."

b. **Ministered by us**: Paul's letter of recommendation was written with a "pen" and the "pen" was Paul himself. He "wrote into" the lives of the people he served.

c. **Written not with ink but by the Spirit of the living God**: Paul's letter of recommendation was written with "ink," and the "ink" was the Holy Spirit.

d. **On tablets of flesh, that is, of the heart**: Paul's letter of recommendation was written on "paper" or **tablets**, and the "paper" was the hearts of the Corinthian Christians.

i. The Old Testament prophets looked forward to the New Covenant, when the law of God would be written in our hearts (Jeremiah 31:33), and said God would grant hearts of flesh to replace hearts of stone (Ezekiel 11:19 and 36:26).

3. (4-6) Sufficient ministers of a new covenant.

And we have such trust through Christ toward God. Not that we are sufficient of ourselves to think of anything as *being* from ourselves, but our sufficiency *is* from God, who also made us sufficient as ministers of the new covenant, not of the letter but of the Spirit; for the letter kills, but the Spirit gives life.

a. **We have such trust through Christ toward God**: Paul knows that what he has just written might sound proud in the ears of the Corinthian Christians. After all, it is no small thing to say, "You are my letter of recommendation" and "I am a pen in God's hand." Paul knows these are big ideas, but his place for thinking these big ideas is in Jesus, not in himself.

b. **Not that we are sufficient of ourselves**: Paul doesn't consider himself **sufficient** for the great task of changing lives for Jesus. Only Jesus is sufficient for such a big job.

i. Some people refuse to be used by God because they think of themselves as "not ready," but in a sense, we are never ready or worthy. If we were, the sufficiency would be in ourselves and not from God.

ii. "Brethren, if Paul is not sufficient of himself, what are you and I? Where are you . . . Do you indulge the dream of self-sufficiency? Be ashamed of your folly in the presence of a great man who knew what he said, and who spoke under the direction of the Spirit of God, and wrote deliberately, 'Not that we are sufficient of ourselves.'" (Spurgeon)

iii. "Our sufficiency is of God; let us practically enjoy this truth. We are poor, leaking vessels, and the only way for us to keep full is to put our pitcher under the perpetual flow of boundless grace. Then, despite its leakage, the cup will always be full to the brim." (Spurgeon)

c. **Ministers of the new covenant**: The idea of a **new covenant** was prophesied in the Old Testament (Jeremiah 31:31) and put into practice by Jesus (Luke 22:19-20).

i. The ancient Greek word for **covenant** (*diatheke*) had the ordinary meaning of a "last will and testament." Paul's use of the word reinforces the sovereignty of God, because it is not a negotiated settlement, but a divine decree.

ii. The word **covenant** describes "An 'arrangement' made by one party with plenary power, which the other party may accept or reject, but cannot alter . . . A covenant offered by God to man was no 'compact' between two parties coming together on equal terms." (Moulton and Milligan)

iii. This **new covenant** presents the terms by which we can have a relationship with God, centered on Jesus and His work for us.

d. **Not of the letter but of the Spirit**: When Paul contrasts **the letter** and **the Spirit**, he isn't favoring "experience" over "the word," nor is he favoring allegorical interpretation over a literal understanding of the Bible. Rather Paul shows the superiority of the **new covenant** over the old covenant.

i. The **letter** is the law in its outward sense, written on tablets of stone. The letter of the law came by the old covenant. It was good in itself, but it gave us no power to serve God, and it did not change our heart; it simply told us what to do. Paul can say **the letter kills** because the law, exposing our guilt, "**kills**" us before God. The law thoroughly and completely establishes our guilt.

ii. Paul expresses this point well in Romans 7:5-6: *For when we were in the flesh, the sinful passions which were aroused by the law were at work in our members to bear fruit to death. But now we have been delivered from the law, having died to what we were held by, so that we should serve in the newness of the Spirit and not in the oldness of the letter.*

iii. The indwelling **Spirit** then becomes for us a law written on our hearts. He is in us to guide us and be our "law." It isn't that the Holy Spirit *replaces* the written law, but *completes* and *fulfills* the work of the written law in our hearts. **The Spirit gives life**, and with this spiritual life, we can live out the law of God.

iv. Therefore, we can't throw away or neglect our Bibles (which some might say is **the letter**) because now we have **the Spirit**. Instead, **the Spirit** makes us alive to **the letter**, *fulfilling* and *completing* the work of **the letter** in us. We also shouldn't think this is permission to live our Christian life on experiences or mystical interpretations of the Bible. Experiences and allegories in the Bible have their place, but each must be proved true and supported by studying the literal meaning of the Bible. **The Spirit** and **the letter** are not enemies, but friends. They don't work against each other, and one is incomplete without the other.

B. A contrast between the old and new covenants.

1. (7-11) The surpassing glory of the new covenant.

But if the ministry of death, written *and* engraved on stones, was glorious, so that the children of Israel could not look steadily at the face of Moses because of the glory of his countenance, which *glory* was passing away, how will the ministry of the Spirit not be more glorious? For if the ministry of condemnation *had* glory, the ministry of righteousness

exceeds much more in glory. For even what was made glorious had no glory in this respect, because of the glory that excels. For if what is passing away *was* glorious, what remains *is* much more glorious.

a. **The ministry of death**: Was it wrong to call the old covenant **the ministry of death**? No, because that is what the law does to us: It slays us as guilty sinners before God so that we can be resurrected by the new covenant. It isn't that the problem was with the law, but with us: *The sinful passions which were aroused by the law were at work in our members to bear fruit to death.* (Romans 7:5)

> i. Trapp on **the ministry of death**: "David was the voice of the law awarding death to sin, 'He shall surely die.' Nathan was the voice of the gospel awarding life to repentance for sin, 'Thou shalt not die.' "

b. **Was glorious**: There was glory associated with the giving of the law and the old covenant. At that time, Mount Sinai was surrounded with smoke; there were earthquakes, thunder, lightning, a trumpet blast from heaven, and the voice of God Himself (Exodus 19:16-20:1). Most of all, the glory of the old covenant was shown in **the face of Moses** and the **glory of his countenance**.

> i. "And although the gospel came not into the world as the law, with thunder, lightning, and earthquakes; yet that was ushered in by angels, foretelling the birth and office of John the Baptist, and of Christ; by the great sign of the virgin's conceiving and bringing forth a Son; by a voice from heaven, proclaiming Christ the Father's only begotten Son, in whom he was well pleased." (Poole)

c. **The face of Moses**: Exodus 34:29-35 describes how Moses put a veil over his face after speaking to the people. As glorious as the radiant face of Moses was, it was a fading glory: **which glory was passing away**. The glory of the old covenant shining through the face of Moses was a fading glory, but the glory of the new covenant endures *without* fading.

d. **How will the ministry of the Spirit not be more glorious**: If the *old* covenant, which brought *death* had this glory, we should expect *greater glory* in the new covenant, which brings **the ministry of the Spirit** and life.

> i. The old covenant was **a ministry of condemnation**, but the new covenant is **the ministry of righteousness**. The old covenant **is passing away**, but the new covenant **remains**. No wonder the new covenant is **much more glorious**!

> ii. The old covenant **had glory**, but the glory of the new covenant far outshines it, just as the sun always outshines the brightest moon. Compared to the new covenant, the old covenant **had no glory** because of **the glory that excels** in the new covenant.

2. (12-16) The open and bold character of the new covenant.

Therefore, since we have such hope, we use great boldness of speech; unlike Moses, *who* put a veil over his face so that the children of Israel could not look steadily at the end of what was passing away. But their minds were blinded. For until this day the same veil remains unlifted in the reading of the Old Testament, because the *veil* is taken away in Christ. But even to this day, when Moses is read, a veil lies on their heart. Nevertheless when one turns to the Lord, the veil is taken away.

a. **Therefore, since we have such hope**: Since our hope is in a more glorious covenant, we can have a more glorious **hope**. Because of this hope, Paul can **use great boldness of speech**. The old covenant restricted and separated men from God; the new covenant brings us to God and enables us to come *boldly* to Him.

b. **Unlike Moses, who put a veil over his face**: Even Moses did not have real boldness under the old covenant. A **veil** is not a "bold" thing to wear; it is a barrier and something to hide behind. Moses lacked boldness (compared to Paul) because the covenant that he ministered under was fading away and fading in glory.

c. **So that the children of Israel could not look steadily at the end of what was passing away**: From reading the account in Exodus 34:29-35, one might first get the impression that Moses wore a veil after his meetings with God so that the people wouldn't be afraid to come near him; the veil was to protect *them* from seeing the shining face of Moses. Here Paul explains the real purpose of the veil: not to hide the shining face of Moses, but to hide the *diminishing* glory of his face because the glory was fading. The **passing** glory of the old covenant contrasts with the enduring glory of the new covenant.

d. **Could not look**: Since the veil hid the face of Moses, the children of Israel couldn't see *any* of the glory from his face. Therefore, the contrast isn't only between **passing** glory and enduring glory, but also between *concealed* glory and *revealed* glory.

e. **For until this day the same veil remains unlifted**: Paul says that most of the Jews of his day could not see that the glory of Moses' ministry faded in comparison to the ministry of Jesus. Because the **veil remains unlifted**, they can't see that the glory of Moses' ministry has faded and they should now look to Jesus. Since the **same veil** that hid Moses' face now **lies on their heart**, they still think there is something superior or more glorious in the ministry of Moses.

f. **Nevertheless, when one turns to the Lord, the veil is taken away**: Paul could say of his fellow Jews that **a veil lies on their heart**, but he

2 Corinthians 3   37

could also say that the veil can be taken away in Jesus. Paul knew this well because he was once veiled to the glory and superiority of Jesus.

> i. Many Christians with a heart to preach to their Jewish friends wonder why it is rarely so simple as just showing them that Jesus is the Messiah. This is because **a veil lies on their heart**. Unless God does a work in them so they turn to the Lord and have the veil taken away, they will never see the fading glory of Moses' covenant and the surpassing glory of Jesus and the new covenant.

> ii. Of course, it could be said that the Jews are not the only ones with **a veil . . . on their heart**. Gentiles also have "veils" that separate them from seeing Jesus and His work for us clearly, and Jesus is more than able to take those veils away. This points to the essential need of *prayer* in evangelism. It has been rightly said that it is more important to talk to God about men than it is to talk to men about God, but we can do both of these important works.

3. (17) The liberty of the new covenant.

Now the Lord is the Spirit; and where the Spirit of the Lord *is*, there *is* liberty.

> a. **The Lord is the Spirit**: From the context of Exodus 34:34, we see that when Paul says **the Lord is the Spirit**, he means that the Holy Spirit is God, just as Jesus and the Father are God.

> b. **Where the Spirit of the Lord is, there is liberty**. Paul's thinking follows like this: When Moses went into God's presence, he had the liberty to take off the veil; the presence of the Lord gave him this liberty. We have the Holy Spirit, who is the Lord. We live in the Spirit's presence because He is given to us under the new covenant. So, just as Moses had the liberty to relate to God without the veil in the presence of the Lord, so we have **liberty** because of the presence of the Holy Spirit.

> > i. We should also consider what Paul is *not* saying. He is not giving license to any Pentecostal or Charismatic excess because **where the Spirit of the Lord is, there is liberty**. We have great liberty in our relationship with God through what Jesus did and through what the Holy Spirit is doing, but we never have the **liberty** to disobey what the Spirit says in the word of God. That is a perversion of true liberty, not a Spirit-led liberty.

> c. **There is liberty**: Paul really has in mind the *liberty of access*. He is building on what he wrote in 2 Corinthians 3:12: *We use great boldness of speech*. Boldness is a word that belongs with **liberty**. Because of the great work of the Holy Spirit in us through the new covenant, we have a bold, liberated relationship with God.

i. "A liberty from the yoke of the law, from sin, death, hell; but the liberty which seemeth here to be chiefly intended, is a liberty from that blindness and hardness which is upon men's hearts, until they have received the Holy Spirit." (Poole)

4. (18) The transforming glory of the new covenant.

But we all, with unveiled face, beholding as in a mirror the glory of the Lord, are being transformed into the same image from glory to glory, just as by the Spirit of the Lord.

a. **We all with unveiled face**: Paul invites every Christian to a special, glorious intimacy with God. This is a relationship and transforming power that is not the property of just a few privileged Christians. It can belong to **all**, to everyone who has an **unveiled face**.

i. How do we get an **unveiled face**? *When one turns to the Lord, the veil is taken away* (2 Corinthians 3:16). If we will turn to the Lord, He will take away the veil and we can be one of the "**we all**."

b. **Beholding as in a mirror the glory of the Lord**: We can see **the glory of the Lord**, but we cannot see His glory perfectly. **A mirror** in the ancient world did not give nearly as good a reflection as our mirrors do today. Ancient mirrors were made of polished metal, and gave a clouded, fuzzy, somewhat distorted image. Paul says, "We can see **the glory of the Lord**, but we can't see it perfectly yet."

i. There may be another thought here also: "Now as *mirrors*, among the Jews, Greeks, and Romans, were made of highly polished *metal*, it would often happen, especially in strong light, that the face would be greatly *illuminated* by this strongly *reflected* light; and to this circumstance the apostle seems here to allude." (Clarke)

c. **Are being transformed**: As we behold the glory of God, we will be **transformed**. God will change our lives and change us from the inside out. Though the old covenant had its glory, it could never transform lives through the law. God uses the new covenant to make us **transformed** people, not just *nice* people.

i. Everyone wants to know, "How can I change?" Or, everyone wants to know, "How can *they* change?" The best and most enduring change comes into our life when we are **transformed** by time spent with the Lord. There are other ways to change, such as guilt, willpower, or coercion, but none of these methods bring change that is as deep and lasts as long as the transformation that comes by the Spirit of God as we spend time in the presence of the Lord.

ii. Yet, it requires something: **beholding**. The word means more than a casual look; it means to make a careful study. We all have something to behold, something to study. We can be transformed by the glory of the Lord, but only if we will *carefully study* it.

d. **Into the same image**: As we look into "God's mirror," we are changed **into the same image** of the Lord. When we spend time **beholding** the glory of the God of love, grace, peace, and righteousness, we will see a transforming growth in love, grace, peace, and righteousness.

i. Of course, this is how you can know someone is really spending time with the Lord: They **are being transformed into the same image**. However, much depends on what we "see" when we look into "God's mirror." In this analogy, "God's mirror" is not a mirror that shows us what *we are* as much as it shows us what *we will become*, and what we will become is based on our picture of who God is. If we have a false picture of God, we will see that false picture in God's "mirror" and will be transformed into that **same image** - much to our harm, both for now and eternity.

ii. Not everyone sees the truth when they look into the mirror. Thirty year-old David gets up every morning, and his morning routine only gets as far as the bedroom mirror, where he sees a horribly distorted face - a crooked, swollen nose covered with scars and a bulging eye. The pain from his deformities made him quit college and move in with his parents ten years ago. Since then, he rarely leaves his room, afraid to let anyone see him. His four cosmetic surgeries have done nothing to help his condition because the problems with David's appearance are only in his *mind*. Experts call it *body dysmorphic disorder*, or BDD. It causes people to imagine themselves as deformed, ugly people when they really have a normal appearance. Psychiatrists call it a hidden epidemic, and one psychiatrist said, "Patients are virtually coming out of the woodwork. I'm meeting with one new patient each week." Most BDD sufferers are convinced the problem is with their face. Those afflicted live with such an overwhelming sense of shame that they can barely function. One young teacher in Boston tried to continue her job but often ran out in the middle of class, afraid that her imagined hideous appearance showed through her thick makeup. A Denver businessman called his mother from the office 15 times a day for reassurance that he did not look grotesque and spent hours in the bathroom stall with a pocket mirror trying to figure out a way to improve his appearance. Some try to cope with harmful rituals, such as cutting themselves to "bleed" the damaged area. BDD sufferers are usually convinced that the problem is with their body, not their mind.

They don't want to see anyone but plastic surgeons and dermatologists for their problem.

iii. Thankfully, we don't have to be in bondage to a false image of ourselves or of God. When we **behold** the picture of God as He is in truth, we will be transformed into His image. This is God's great design in our salvation, *for whom He foreknew, He also predestined to be conformed to the image of His Son* (Romans 8:29). Calvin speaks to this great design of God: "That the image of God, which has been defaced by sin, may be repaired within us . . . the progress of this restoration is continuous through the whole of life, because it is little by little that God causes His glory to shine forth in us."

e. **Are being transformed**: This work of transformation is a process. We are **being** transformed; the work isn't complete yet, and no one should expect it to be complete in themselves or in others. No one comes away from one incredible time with the Lord perfectly **transformed**.

f. **From glory to glory**: The work of transformation is a continual progression. It works **from glory to glory**. It doesn't have to work from *backsliding to glory to backsliding to glory*. God's work in our lives can be a continual progression, **from glory to glory**.

g. **By the Spirit of the Lord**: With these last words, Paul emphasizes two things. First, this access to God and His transforming presence is ours by the new covenant, because it is through the new covenant we are given **the Spirit of the Lord**. Secondly, this work of transformation really is God's work in us. It happens **by the Spirit of the Lord**, not by the will or effort of man. We don't *achieve* or *earn* spiritual transformation by **beholding as in a mirror the glory of the Lord**. We simply put ourselves in a place where **the Spirit of the Lord** can transform us.

2 Corinthians 4 - Our Light Affliction

A. How a more glorious covenant should be presented.

1. (1-2) How Paul preached the more glorious gospel.

Therefore, since we have this ministry, as we have received mercy, we do not lose heart. But we have renounced the hidden things of shame, not walking in craftiness nor handling the word of God deceitfully, but by manifestation of the truth commending ourselves to every man's conscience in the sight of God.

a. **Since we have this ministry . . . we do not lose heart**: Paul preached his gospel *boldly*. When Paul considered the greatness of his calling, it gave him the heart to face all his difficulties. We often **lose heart** because we do not consider how great a calling God gives us in Jesus.

i. The idea behind the ancient Greek word for "**lose heart**" is of the "faint-hearted coward." The ancient Greek word has the connotation of not only a lack of courage but of bad behavior and evil conduct.

ii. "The preacher should either speak in God's name or hold his tongue. My brother, if the Lord has not sent you with a message, go to bed, or to school, or mind your farm; for what does it matter what you have to say of your own? If heaven has given you a message, speak it out as he ought to speak who is called to be the mouth of God." (Spurgeon)

b. **As we have received mercy**: Paul preached his gospel *humbly*. He knew his glorious calling to ministry was not due to his own works but by **mercy**. Mercy, by its very nature, is undeserved.

c. **Renounced the hidden things of shame, not walking in craftiness nor handling the word of God deceitfully**: Paul preached his gospel *honestly*. The ancient Greek word translated to **deceitfully** is a verb only found here in the New Testament, meaning "to dilute or adulterate." Paul didn't preach a *concealed* gospel (**renouncing the hidden things of shame**) or a *corrupted* gospel (**craftiness . . . deceitfully**), mixing the message with human ingenuity or watering it down to accommodate his audience. Paul preached an *honest* gospel.

> i. Many preachers fail on this exact point. They have the true gospel, but they *add to it* things of human ingenuity and wisdom. Often, they add these corrupting or diluting things to the gospel because they think adding them will make the gospel more effective or give it a greater hearing. They are still doing what Paul insisted he would never do, **handling the word of God deceitfully**.

> ii. "Certain divines tell us that they must adapt truth to the advance of the age, which means that they must murder it and fling its dead body to the dogs . . . which simply means that a popular lie shall take the place of an offensive truth." (Spurgeon)

> iii. **Craftiness** speaks of "a cunning readiness to adopt any device or trickery for the achievement of ends which are anything but altruistic." (Hughes)

d. **By manifestation of the truth**: Paul preached an *openly true* gospel. Anyone could look at what Paul preached and see the plain truth of it. He did not preach an elaborate system of hidden mysteries.

e. **Commending ourselves to every man's conscience**: Paul preached a gospel of *integrity*. Anyone could look at Paul's gospel and ministry, then judge it by his or her own conscience and see that it was full of integrity.

> i. Some men attacked Paul with *words* and some attacked him with *actions*. Nevertheless, Paul knew both his ministry and his message found approval in the **conscience** of every man, even if he would not admit it.

f. **In the sight of God**: Paul preached his gospel *before God*. It was important to Paul to know **every man's conscience** would approve his manner of ministry, but it was far more important to know that what he did was right **in the sight of God**.

> i. "There is a higher scrutiny than that of the human conscience: It is to *God* that every minister of the gospel is ultimately and eternally answerable." (Hughes)

> ii. Later in this chapter, Paul will reflect again on his sufferings. In these first two verses, he makes it clear that he did not suffer because he has been an unfaithful minister of the gospel. It was easy for Paul's enemies to claim, "He suffers so much because God is punishing him for his unfaithfulness," but that wasn't true at all.

2. (3-4) Why don't more people respond to such a glorious gospel?

But even if our gospel is veiled, it is veiled to those who are perishing, whose minds the god of this age has blinded, who do not believe, lest the light of the gospel of the glory of Christ, who is the image of God, should shine on them.

a. **Even if our gospel is veiled, it is veiled to those who are perishing**: If people do not respond to this glorious gospel, it isn't Paul's fault or his gospel's fault. Only those who are perishing miss the message.

i. "The blindness of unbelievers in no way detracts from the clearness of the gospel for the sun is no less resplendent because the blind do not perceive its light." (Calvin)

ii. The King James Version translates the end of verse four: *hid to them that are lost.* Spurgeon well says, "According to the text, he that believes not on Jesus Christ is a lost man. God has lost you; you are not his servant. The church has lost you; you are not working for the truth. The world has lost you really; you yield no lasting service to it. You have lost yourself to right, to joy, to heaven. You are lost, lost, lost.. It is not only that you *will be* lost, but that you *are* lost . . . lost even now."

b. **Whose minds the god of this age has blinded**: Those **who are perishing** and for whom the **gospel is veiled** have been **blinded** by Satan, **the god of this age**.

i. It doesn't mean they are *innocent victims* of Satan's blinding work. Satan's work upon them is not the *only* reason they are blinded. John 3:19 says, *this is the condemnation, that the light has come into the world, and men loved darkness rather than light, because their deeds were evil.* Though men *love* the darkness, and *choose* the darkness, Satan still works hard to *keep* them **blinded** to the glorious gospel of light and salvation in Jesus.

ii. We notice also that it is the **minds** of the unbelieving that are **blinded**. Of course, Satan also works on the *heart* and the *emotions* of the lost, but his main battleground is the *mind.* Can't we see a strategy of Satan in working hard to make people *think* less and *learn* less and use their **minds** less? This also is why God has chosen the *word* to transmit the gospel, because the *word* touches our **minds** and can touch **minds the god of this age has blinded**.

c. **The god of this age**: The title **god of this age** is not used of Satan anywhere else in Scripture, but the thought is expressed in passages like John 12:31, John 14:30, Ephesians 2:2, Ephesians 6:12 and 1 John 5:19.

i. There is a significant and real sense in which Satan "rules" this world. Not in an ultimate sense, because, *the earth is the Lord's, and all its fullness, the world and those who dwell therein* (Psalm 24:1). Yet, Jesus did not contest Satan's claim to rule over this present age (Luke 4:5-8), because there is a sense in which Satan is the "popularly elected" ruler of **this age**.

ii. "The satanic world sovereignty is in fact apparent rather than real; for God alone is the 'King of the ages' (1 Timothy 1:17, Greek), that is, of every age, past, present, and future" (Hughes). "It is the devil who is here called *the god of this world*, because he ruleth over the greatest part of the world, and they are his servants and slaves . . . though we no where else find him called the god of this world, yet our Saviour twice calls him *the prince of this world*." (Poole)

iii. The Biblical truth that Satan is **the god of this age** can be understood in a wrong way. Some later Christians (like the Manichaeans) promoted a dualistic understanding of God and Satan, and emphasized this phrase **the god of this age**. Their idea was that God and Satan were "equal opponents," instead of understanding that in no way is Satan the opposite of God. In reaction to these false doctrines, many early Christian commentators (like Augustine, Origen, Chrysostem, and others) interpreted this verse strangely to "remove ammunition" from the heretics. But this is wrong. Just because someone twists a truth one way, it doesn't mean we can twist it the other way to "compensate." Calvin well remarks of this approach, "being hard pressed by their opponents they were more anxious to refute them than to expound Paul."

iv. Instead, Calvin gives a good sense of what we should understand by the phrase **the god of this age**: "The devil is called the god of this age in no other way than Baal was called the god of those who worshipped him or the dog the god of Egypt."

d. **Who do not believe**: Satan can only blind those **who do not believe**. If you are tired of having your mind **blinded** by **the god of this age**, then put your trust in who Jesus is and what He did for you. Then Satan can't blind you anymore.

i. "The god of this world is able only to blind the minds of the unbelieving . . . Refusal to believe is the secret and reason of the blindness that happens to men." (Morgan)

e. **Lest the light of the gospel of the glory of Christ . . . should shine on them**: To see this glory is to be saved. Therefore, Satan directs his energies into blinding men from ever seeing **the light of the gospel of the glory of Christ**.

i. Understanding Satan's strategy with unbelievers should affect how we pray for the lost. We should ask God to shine His light, to bind the blinding work of Satan, and to give faith to overcome the unbelief that invites the blinding.

f. Paul knew what he was talking about when he wrote this. He himself was completely blind to the truth until God broke through the darkness. In fact, when Paul first encountered Jesus, the Lord struck him with a literal blindness that was healed, and his eyes - both spiritually and physically - were opened to see the glory of Jesus Christ (Acts 9:1-19).

i. The **light** mentioned here isn't the normal ancient Greek word for light. It is a word used in the Septuagint in Psalm 44:3 for *the light of Your countenance* and in Psalm 78:14 for *In the daytime also He led them with the cloud, and all the night with a light of fire.* Hodge observes, "The word therefore signifies the brightness emitted by a radiant body."

B. Treasure in clay pots.

1. (5-6) The topic of Paul's preaching: Jesus, not self.

For we do not preach ourselves, but Christ Jesus the Lord, and ourselves your bondservants for Jesus' sake. For it is the God who commanded light to shine out of darkness, who has shone in our hearts to *give* the light of the knowledge of the glory of God in the face of Jesus Christ.

a. **For we do not preach ourselves**: Paul didn't climb into the pulpit or stand before an audience to preach himself. He wasn't important and he wasn't the focus. Jesus was the focus, so Paul could strongly say, **we do not preach ourselves**. Instead, the focus must be on **Christ Jesus the Lord**. He is the one to preach about!

i. Not everyone who opens a Bible and starts talking is preaching **Christ Jesus the Lord**. Many well-intentioned preachers actually preach themselves instead of Jesus. If the focus is on the funny stories or the touching life experiences of the preacher, he may be preaching himself.

ii. Often, people love it when the preacher preaches himself. It seems revealing and intimate, and it is often entertaining. It is also tempting for the preacher because he sees how people respond when he focuses the message on himself. Nevertheless, the bottom line is that the preacher himself can't bring you to God and save your eternal soul; only Jesus can. So preach Jesus!

iii. Is it wrong for a preacher to tell a joke or to use a story from his own life? Of course not, but it is all a matter of proportion. It's like asking, "Is it all right to put salt in the soup?" Of course, but don't put in too much. And if week after week too much of the preacher is in the sermon, it is wrong. A.T. Robertson said the preaching of one's self was "Surely as poor and disgusting a topic as a preacher can find." Don't we have a greater message than ourselves?

b. **But Christ Jesus the Lord**: It wasn't only that Paul did *not* preach himself. He also did not preach a gospel of moral reform or a list of rules you must follow to be right with God. He preached Jesus, presenting **Christ Jesus the Lord**.

i. Paul's goal in preaching was to bring men to Jesus, not to make moral changes in men. "To make the end of preaching the inculcation of virtue, to render men honest, sober, benevolent and faithful, is part and parcel of that wisdom of the world that is foolishness with God. It is attempting to raise fruit without trees. When a man is brought to recognize Jesus Christ as Lord, and to love and worship him as such, then he becomes like Christ. What more can the moralist want?" (Hodge)

c. **Ourselves your servants for Jesus' sake**: When Paul *did* present himself, this is how he did it. Not as a lord, not as a master, but simply as **your servants for Jesus' sake**.

i. It is important that Paul also considered himself a servant of the Corinthian Christians **for Jesus' sake**. If it were for his own sake or for the sake of the Corinthian Christians themselves, it wouldn't last or it would turn fleshly pretty easily. Paul always served others **for Jesus' sake**. He did it primarily to please Jesus, not to please man.

d. **The God who commanded light to shine out of darkness**: Paul is saying, "The Lord God who created light in the physical world can fill your heart with spiritual light, even if you are blinded by the god of this age." Satan's work of blinding is great, but God's work of bringing light is greater.

i. Paul directly quotes the idea of Genesis 1:3: *Then God said, "Let there be light"; and there was light*. Paul *really believed* the account of creation as described in Genesis 1. Genesis 1:3 says that God created light with a command, and Paul believed that is *exactly* how it happened.

e. **Who has shone in our hearts**: This describes Paul's own conversion accurately (Acts 9:1-9). On his was to Damascus to persecute and kill Christians, *suddenly a light shone around him from heaven*. This was the first encounter with Jesus in the life of Saul of Tarsus (also known later as the Apostle Paul).

i. This should be a good way to describe every Christian: *people with shining hearts*. God **shone in our hearts**, and it should show in shining lives for Jesus Christ.

f. To give us the light of the knowledge of the glory of God: What exactly has God **shone in our hearts?** It is **the light of the knowledge of the glory of God**. Every Christian should have *some* knowledge of the glory of God. If one is a Christian and can say, "I really know nothing of the **light of the knowledge of the glory of God**," then he or she should seek God earnestly so that He would shine it in their heart.

i. **To give us the light**: God gives us the light of the knowledge of God, and we have the responsibility to get it out. He "shined it in" so that we could "shine it out" instead of "shining it on" as some Christians seem to do.

ii. Imagine a man in a sunny room who enjoys the sunshine so much he wants to keep it all to himself. He says, "I'll shut the curtains so that none of this light gets out!" and puts himself back into darkness. When we try to hoard up the light within ourselves, we will certainly lose it.

g. In the face of Jesus Christ: We come to **the knowledge of the glory of God** by seeing it **in the face of Jesus**. God gave us a display, a picture, a representation of His glory: His Son, Jesus Christ. Jesus said, *He who has seen Me has seen the Father* (John 14:9). He also prayed that we would see His glory, the glory of God the Father: *that they may behold My glory which You have given Me* (John 17:24).

2. (7) A great treasure in such a humble container.

But we have this treasure in earthen vessels, that the excellence of the power may be of God and not of us.

a. **This treasure**: The **treasure** is the greatness of the gospel of Jesus Christ, and the glory of God made evident through that gospel. It is the very *light* of God and the *light of the knowledge of the glory of God*, reflected in the *face of Jesus Christ*. This is the greatest **treasure** in all creation!

b. **We have this treasure in earthen vessels**: When Paul considers us as **earthen vessels**, he isn't disparaging the body or considering it merely a receptacle for the soul. Instead, Paul simply compares the "value" of God's light and glory and the "value" of what He chose to put His light and glory into. When you compare the two, it isn't hard to be amazed that God has put such a great **treasure** into clay pots.

i. Who is *worthy* to be a "container" for God's light and glory? The smartest person isn't smart enough, the purest person isn't pure enough, the most spiritual person isn't spiritual enough, and the most talented person isn't talented enough. We are all just clay pots holding an unspeakably great treasure.

ii. **Earthen vessels**: Earthenware vessels were common in every home in the ancient world. They were not very durable (compared to metal), and they were useless if broken (glass could be melted down again). "They were thus cheap and of little intrinsic value." (Kruse) God chose to put His light and glory in the *everyday dishes*, not in the *fine china*.

iii. We almost always are drawn to the thing that has the best *packaging*, but the best gifts often have the most unlikely packaging. God did not see a need to "package" Jesus when He came as a man to this earth. Jesus was not embarrassed to live as an **earthen vessel**. God is not embarrassed to use clay pots like us.

c. **That the excellence of the power may be of God and not of us**: Why does God put such a great treasure in such weak vessels? So that the greatness **of the power may be of God and not of us**. So that it would be evident to anyone who had eyes to see that the work was being done by the power of God, not the power of the vessel.

i. Why did God choose risky, earthen vessels instead of safe, heavenly ones? Because "perfect" vessels are safe but bring glory to themselves. **Earthen vessels** are risky but can bring profound glory to God.

ii. In the story of Gideon, it was the breaking of vessels that made the light shine forth and bring victory to God's people (Judges 7:20). In the rest of the chapter, Paul will show how God "breaks" His clay pots so that **the excellence of the power may be of God and not of us**.

3. (8-12) The suffering in Paul's ministry brought forth life.

We are **hard pressed on every side, yet not crushed;** *we are* **perplexed, but not in despair; persecuted, but not forsaken; struck down, but not destroyed; always carrying about in the body the dying of the Lord Jesus, that the life of Jesus also may be manifested in our body. For we who live are always delivered to death for Jesus' sake, that the life of Jesus also may be manifested in our mortal flesh. So then death is working in us, but life in you.**

a. **We are hard pressed**: This has the idea of "hunted." Paul was a wanted, hunted man because of what he was for Jesus. In Acts 23:12, 40 men conspired together to not eat or drink until they had murdered Paul. Paul knew what it was like to be hunted.

b. **Yet not crushed**: Living as a wanted, hunted man means terrible stress, experienced every moment of the day. Yet Paul was **not crushed** by this stress. He could still serve the Lord gloriously.

c. **Hard pressed . . . perplexed . . . persecuted . . . struck down**: Paul's life was hard, and it was hard because of his passionate devotion to Jesus Christ and His gospel. Yet look at the triumph of Jesus in Paul's life: **not crushed . . . not in despair . . . not forsaken . . . not destroyed**. Paul knew the power and victory of Jesus in his life because he was continually in situations where only the power and victory of Jesus could meet his need.

> i. When we talk about suffering like this today, it is easy to think we are just saying "spiritual things," because some of us live very comfortable lives and do not suffer much at all. Nevertheless, we should remember that everything Paul said about suffering, he said as a man who probably suffered more than you or anyone you will ever meet. This was not theory to Paul but real life experience.

d. **Always carrying about in the body the dying of the Lord Jesus, that the life of Jesus also may be manifested**: Paul, like any Christian, wanted **the life of Jesus** evident in him. Paul knew this could only happen if he also carried **about in the body the dying of the Lord Jesus**. There are some aspects of God's great work in our lives that only happen through trials and suffering.

> i. By writing **always carrying about in the body the dying of the Lord Jesus**, Paul meant that he felt as if the death of Jesus was being spiritually worked inside of him. He is saying that the death of Jesus was not only a historical fact, it also was a spiritual reality in his life.

> ii. In Philippians 3:10, Paul speaks about the glory of knowing Jesus: *that I may know Him and the power of His resurrection, and the fellowship of His sufferings, being conformed to His death.* Many long to know *the power of His resurrection* but want nothing to do with *the fellowship of His sufferings* or *being conformed to His death*. However, there are certain fragrances God can only release through a broken vial, so Paul rejoiced in knowing both the suffering and the glory. He knew the two were connected.

e. **Always delivered to death . . . death is working in us, but life in you**: Paul knew the spiritual riches that he brought to the Corinthian Christians came in part through the death-like suffering he endured in ministry. God made Paul more effective in ministry through his suffering.

> i. Sometimes we think that if someone is really spiritual or really used of God they will live in a constant state of "victory" that means life will always be easy. Understanding what Paul wrote here not only tells us that God's servants may experience death-like suffering but that *God has a good and glorious purpose* in allowing it.

ii. G. Campbell Morgan tells the story of a great young preacher who was impressive early in his ministry. Once he had the young man to speak at his church, and after the sermon Morgan asked his wife, "Wasn't that wonderful?" She quietly replied, "Yes, but it will be more wonderful when he has suffered." Morgan adds: "Well, he suffered, and it *was* more powerful."

f. **Death in us, but life in you**: Here is the irony. The Corinthian Christians despised Paul because of his great sufferings and because of what they thought was their great lives of "victory." They did not see that their lives of victory were only possible because God made Paul such an effective servant through suffering.

i. "Very good interpreters think these words a smart ironical expression, by which the apostle reflecteth upon a party in this church who from his sufferings concluded against the truth of his doctrine, or his favour with God." (Poole)

4. (13-15) Paul's faith in the life-giving God.

And since we have the same spirit of faith, according to what is written, "I believed and therefore I spoke," we also believe and therefore speak, knowing that He who raised up the Lord Jesus will also raise us up with Jesus, and will present *us* with you. For all things *are* for your sakes, that grace, having spread through the many, may cause thanksgiving to abound to the glory of God.

a. **We also believe and therefore speak**: This is a great principle - that faith creates the testimony. Paul *really believed* God had a purpose in his death-like sufferings, and *really believed* he lived and experienced the resurrection life of Jesus. Therefore, he wasn't hesitant to **speak** about it.

i. If you can't say "**we also believe**," then you should not **speak**. "That is one great secret of power and success in the Christian ministry. If you do not believe, shut your mouth. That is a word for young ministers. If you do not believe, do not talk." (Morgan)

b. **Knowing that He who raised up the Lord Jesus will also raise us up with Jesus**: Paul *knew* this; therefore, he didn't despair in his sufferings. Every death-like trial was just the prelude to resurrection power.

c. **All things are for your sakes**: This was the immediate goal of Paul's ministry. His heart was to serve the Corinthian Christians and the Christians in other cities. Paul's ministry also had an ultimate goal, that it **may cause thanksgiving to abound to the glory of God**. Ultimately, Paul was motivated by the **glory of God**.

i. Some forget the *immediate goal* and have a "pie-in-the-sky" super-spirituality. Others forget the *ultimate goal* and are man-focused, becoming either proud or discouraged. We need to keep both in mind, just as Paul did.

C. Our light affliction.

1. (16) Why we do not lose heart.

Therefore we do not lose heart. Even though our outward man is perishing, yet the inward *man* is being renewed day by day.

a. **Therefore we do not lose heart**: Paul began the chapter (2 Corinthians 4:1) by declaring *since we have this ministry, as we have received mercy, we do not lose heart*. Then in the chapter he described all the death-like sufferings he had to endure in the ministry. It is as if Paul now anticipates the question, "how can you *not* **lose heart?**"

i. **Therefore** is part of the answer, because it points us back to what Paul just wrote. Paul just explained that his death-like trials made for more effective, life giving ministry for the Corinthian Christians. Knowing this made him **not lose heart** in the midst of trials and suffering.

b. **Even though our outward man is perishing, yet the inward man is being renewed day by day**: Another reason why Paul does not **lost heart** is because though all his suffering takes a toll on the **outward man**, yet the **inward man** is being renewed and blessed.

i. **Outward man** has the same idea as *earthen vessels* in 2 Corinthians 4:7 and *mortal flesh* in 2 Corinthians 4:11. The message is the same: "On the outside, we are suffering and taking a beating, but on the inside, God is blessing and renewing us!"

2. (17-18) A coming glory that outweighs any of today's difficulties.

For our light affliction, which is but for a moment, is working for us a far more exceeding *and* eternal weight of glory, while we do not look at the things which are seen, but at the things which are not seen. For the things which are seen *are* temporary, but the things which are not seen *are* eternal.

a. **Our light affliction**: When Paul writes "**our light affliction**," we might wonder if he ever knew any "real" trials. Some might think, "Well Paul, *your* affliction might be light, but mine isn't. If you only knew how I am suffering! Why, it's unbearable!"

i. Paul didn't write as a kindergartner in the school of suffering - he had an advanced graduate degree. He described some of his suffering with these terms in 2 Corinthians 11:23-28:

- *Stripes*
- *Prisons*
- *Beaten*
- *Stoned*
- *Shipwrecked*
- *Perils of waters*
- *Robbers*
- *In perils of my own countrymen*
- *In perils of the Gentiles*
- *In perils in the city*
- *In perils in the wilderness*
- *In perils in the sea*
- *In perils among false brethren*
- *In weariness and toil*
- *In sleeplessness often*
- *In hunger and thirst*
- *In fastings often*
- *In cold and nakedness*

ii. Those were just the physical, outward sufferings - what about the *spiritual* burdens he bore and *spiritual* attacks he faced? "This rich theology of suffering was forged on the anvil of his own experiences of 'the sufferings of Christ.' " (Harris)

iii. So when Paul writes **our light affliction**, we can know God means **our light affliction**. If Paul could say his affliction was **light**, then what is ours?

b. **Our light affliction**: Why is our **affliction** light and not heavy? Because even the worst of it, by the measure of eternity, is **but for a moment**. This is partially true in the sense that most of our troubles come and go, and "this too shall pass." It is also true in the sense that even a long life by this world's standard is *nothing* on the scale of eternity. Even if one were to live for a hundred years and suffer every day, by the measure of eternity it is **but for a moment**.

c. **Our light affliction**: Why is our **affliction** light and not heavy? Because of what God accomplishes in us through our **affliction**: **a far more exceeding and eternal weight of glory**.

i. The Scriptures are clear: *if indeed we suffer with Him, that we may also be glorified together* (Romans 8:17). Glory is tied to suffering, and God will accomplish in us a glory far heavier than any affliction we have suffered here. "Affliction is not something to be endured in order to reach glory. It is the very process which creates the glory. Through travail comes birth." (Morgan)

ii. It is as if Paul says, "Go ahead and get out the scale. Put all your afflictions on one side of the scale, and even put your thumb down on that side. Then let me place the **weight of glory** on the other side of the scale, and you will see what a **light affliction** you really have."

iii. Yes, our **affliction** is **light**!

- Our affliction is light compared to what others suffer

- Our affliction is light compared to what we deserve

- Our affliction is light compared to what Jesus suffered for us

- Our affliction is light compared to the blessings we enjoy

- Our affliction is light as we experience the sustaining power of God's grace

- Our affliction is light when we see the glory that it leads to

iv. Understanding this we really can say with Paul, "**our light affliction.**"

d. **Weight of glory**: It isn't easy to appreciate the **weight of glory** because it is an **eternal weight**. Often, the problem isn't so much in what we think about our **light affliction** but in that we think so little of our coming **weight of glory**.

i. "It is everywhere visible what influence St. Paul's Hebrew had on his Greek: *chabad*, signifies to be *heavy*, and to be *glorious*; the apostle in his Greek unites these two significations, and says, WEIGHT *of* GLORY." (Dodd, cited in Clarke)

e. **We do not look at the things which are seen, but at the things which are not seen**: Paul meant this especially about his own life and ministry. In the world's eyes, Paul's life was an incredible failure. At the height of a career that would reach much higher, he left it all for a life of hardship, suffering and persecution, with eventual martyrdom. Paul recognized that the world only sees the outward, not the unseen eternal things.

i. When we **look at the things which are seen**, all we see is **our light affliction**, and then it doesn't seem very light! But when we look at **the things which are not seen**, then we see and appreciate the **eternal weight of glory**.

ii. Paul isn't saying that all afflictions *automatically* produce glory. It is possible to allow suffering to destroy us and to let affliction make us bitter, miserable, and self-focused. However, if we will look to **the things which are not seen** then our affliction will work in us an **eternal weight of glory**.

2 Corinthians 5 - Ambassadors for Christ

A. The Christian's destiny.

1. (1) Our existence in the world to come.

For we know that if our earthly house, *this* tent, is destroyed, we have a building from God, a house not made with hands, eternal in the heavens.

a. **For we know**: Paul has just contrasted *our light affliction* with *a far more exceeding and eternal weight of glory*, and things which are *seen* and *temporary* with things that are *not seen* and *eternal* (2 Corinthians 4:17-18). Now, Paul will write more about this contrast between the earthly and the eternal.

i. In this discussion, Paul is bold enough to say, **"We know."** Christians can **know** what the world beyond this one is like because we **know** what God's eternal word says.

ii. "Not we think, or hope only; this is the top-gallant of faith, the triumph of trust; this is, as Latimer calls it, the sweet-meats of the feast of a good conscience. There are other dainty dishes in this feast, but this is the banquet." (Trapp)

b. **Our earthly house, this tent**: Paul thinks of our bodies as *tents* - temporary structures that cannot be thought of as the whole person. If the **tent** is **destroyed**, we still have an eternal hope: **a building from God, a house not made with hands, eternal in the heavens.**

i. **Destroyed** is the very same word used for "striking down a tent." One day, God will "strike the tent," and we will each receive a new **building from God**, a place to live in through all eternity.

ii. "Many people are in a great fright about the future, yet here is Paul viewing the worst thing that could happen to him with such complacency that he likens it to nothing worse than the pulling down of tent in which he was making shift to reside for a little season." (Spurgeon)

iii. This means that we are more than our bodies and explains why Paul could consider all the pain and discomfort in his body a *light affliction* compared to the *eternal weight of glory* to come. It is a mistake to say, "My body isn't me." In truth, my body *is* me, but only *part* of me. There is much more to me than this body.

c. Our future bodies are **not made with hands**. God specially makes them to suit the environment of eternity and heaven; they are **eternal in the heavens**.

i. Jesus said, *"In My Father's house are many mansions; if it were not so, I would have told you. I go to prepare a place for you"* (John 14:2). According to the literal wording of the ancient Greek, the word for *mansions* is better translated "dwelling place" or "a place to stay." But in light of God's character, it is better translated *mansions!* This **building from God, a house not made with hands, eternal in the heavens** will be a glorious place to stay, a mansion for all eternity. After all, Jesus has been preparing that place for us since He ascended into heaven.

ii. Salvation isn't just for the soul or spirit, but for the body also. *Resurrection* is how God saves our bodies. We have a glorious new body to come. "The righteous are put into their graves all weary and worn; but as such they will not rise. They go there with the furrowed brow, the hollowed cheek, the wrinkled skin; they shall wake up in beauty and glory." (Spurgeon)

2. (2-4) Our longing for the heavenly body.

For in this we groan, earnestly desiring to be clothed with our habitation which is from heaven, if indeed, having been clothed, we shall not be found naked. For we who are in *this* tent groan, being burdened, not because we want to be unclothed, but further clothed, that mortality may be swallowed up by life.

a. **For in this we groan**: Christians therefore **groan** because we see both the *limitations* of this body and *superiority* of the body to come. We are **earnestly desiring** our new bodies.

i. Many of us are not **earnestly desiring** heaven. Is it because we are so comfortable on earth? It isn't that we should seek out affliction, but neither should we dedicate our lives to the pursuit of comfort. There is nothing wrong with **earnestly desiring** heaven; there is something right about being able to agree with Paul, and saying "**we groan.**"

b. **Earnestly desiring to be clothed . . . having been clothed, we shall not be naked**: Paul is simply saying that in eternity, we will be **clothed** and not be **naked** - that is, we will not be bodiless spirits.

i. The Greek philosophers thought that a bodiless spirit was the highest level of existence. They thought of the body as a prison for the soul, and saw no advantage in being resurrected in another body.

ii. To God, the body itself is not a negative. The problem isn't in the body itself but in *these* sin-corrupted, fallen bodies that we live in. Jesus approved the essential goodness of the body by becoming a man. If there was something inherently evil in the body, Jesus could never have added humanity to His deity.

c. **Not because we want to be unclothed, but further clothed**: As Christians, we have no earnest desire to be "pure spirit" and to escape the body. Instead, we are **earnestly desiring** to have a perfect, resurrected, body.

i. We really don't know all that much about the state of our resurrected bodies. "If after that you desire to know more concerning this house, I can but give you the advice which was given by John Bunyan in a similar case. One asked of honest John a question which he could not answer, for the matter was not opened up in God's word; and therefore honest John bade his friend live a godly life, and go to heaven, *and see for himself.*" (Spurgeon)

d. **That mortality may be swallowed up in life**: Our new bodies will not be subject to death (**mortality**). Instead, as Paul wrote in 1 Corinthians 15:54, *Death is swallowed up in victory.* When we receive our eternal bodies, life completely conquers death. If a snake **swallowed up** a mouse, the mouse is completely conquered; it is no more. Even so, death will **be swallowed up in life**.

e. **But further clothed**: In Medieval times, some Christians who had never been monks were buried in the clothing of a monk, hoping to do a little better on judgment day dressed like a monk. Jesus offers us a far better garment.

3. (5-8) Our confidence.

Now He who has prepared us for this very thing *is* God, who also has given us the Spirit as a guarantee. So *we are* always confident, knowing that while we are at home in the body we are absent from the Lord. For we walk by faith, not by sight. We are confident, yes, well pleased rather to be absent from the body and to be present with the Lord.

a. **Now He who has prepared us**: God is preparing us *right now* for our eternal destiny. Here, Paul connects the ideas of *our light affliction* and the *eternal weight of glory* (2 Corinthians 5:17-18). *Our light affliction* is (in part) how God **has prepared us**.

i. A man in the middle of many painful trials took a walk in his neighborhood and saw a construction crew at work on a big church. He stood and watched a stone craftsman work a long time on a block but could not see where the block would fit, because the church appeared to be finished. He watched the man work on the block carefully and methodically, slowly shaping it into a precise pattern. Finally, he asked, "Why are you spending so much time chipping and shaping that block?" The craftsman pointed up to the top of the nearly completed steeple and said, "I'm shaping it down here so it will fit in up there." The man in the middle of the trials instantly knew that was God's message to him: He was being **prepared** down here so that he would fit in up in heaven.

b. **Who has also given us the Spirit as a guarantee**: When the trials are hard on earth, it isn't always easy to take comfort in our heavenly destiny. God knew this, so He gave **us the Spirit as a guarantee**. He backs up the promise of heaven with a down payment right now, the Holy Spirit.

i. **Guarantee** is the ancient Greek word *arrhabon*, which described a pledge or a partial payment that required future payments but gave the one receiving the **guarantee** a legal claim to the goods in question. In the modern Greek language, *arrhabona* means "engagement ring."

ii. Many Christians experience great blessing from the Holy Spirit right now. When we consider how glorious the down payment is, we should consider how great the whole gift will be.

iii. "So the Holy Spirit is a part of heaven itself. The work of the Holy Spirit in the soul is the bud of heaven. Grace is not a thing which will be taken away from us when we enter glory, but will develop into glory. Grace will not be withdrawn as though it had answered its purpose, but will be matured into glory." (Spurgeon)

c. **Therefore we are always confident**: The presence of the Holy Spirit in Paul's life gave him confidence. It assured him that God was at work in him and would continue His work. If you cannot say of yourself that you **are always confident**, then ask God for a fresh outpouring of the Holy Spirit in your life.

i. We can be **always confident**, even in hard times, if we keep Colossians 3:2: *Set your mind on things above, not on things on the earth.* "What, then, is the way to maintain peace when there are changes in the soul; when we are sometimes taken up to heaven and are anon cast down? Why, the only way is never to be unduly elated by prosperity without or within, and never to be unduly depressed by adversity or by doubts and fears, because you have learned to live neither upon the things without nor upon things within, but upon things above, which are the true food for a new-born spirit." (Spurgeon)

d. **While we are at home in the body we are absent from the Lord. For we walk by faith, not by sight**: Right now, the presence of God is a matter of faith. We are **at home in the body** so there is a sense in which we are **absent from the Lord**, at least in the sense of His immediate, glorious presence. So now, we must **walk by faith, not by sight**.

i. To **walk by faith, not by sight** is one of the great - and difficult - principles of Christian living. It must amaze the angels that we live for, serve, and are willing to die for a God we have never seen. Yet we love Him and live for Him, living **by faith, not by sight**.

ii. To **walk by faith** means to make faith part of every daily activity. *Walking* is nothing remarkable in itself; it is one of the more mundane aspects of life. But God wants us to **walk by faith**. "That man has not yet learned the true spirit of Christianity who is always saying, 'I can preach a sermon by faith.' Yes, sir, but can you make a coat by faith? 'I can distribute tracts, and visit the district by faith.' Can you cook a dinner by faith? I mean, can you perform the common actions of the household, and the daily duties which fall to your lot, in the spirit of faith?" (Spurgeon)

iii. The day will come when we will no longer be **absent from the Lord** in the sense Paul means it here. On that day, we will not have to **walk by faith**, but we will see the glory and the presence of God **by sight**.

e. **We are confident, yes, well pleased rather to be absent from the body and to be present with the Lord**: Because Paul is **confident** (in part, based on the guarantee of the Holy Spirit) of his eternal destiny, he is not afraid of the world beyond. In fact, he would be **well pleased** to be **absent from the body and to be present with the Lord**.

i. This text deals with a question on the minds of many: What happens to believers when they die? Christians will leave these bodies, be resurrected in new bodies, and be with the Lord. Plainly speaking, **to be absent from the body** means we will **be present with the Lord**.

ii. But will we live in heaven for a time in an intermediate, bodiless state awaiting resurrection? Some think so, based on passages like Revelation 6:9-11 and 1 Thessalonians 4:16. But here, Paul seems to see such a bodiless state as undesirable. Either the present dead in Christ are with the Lord in a spiritual body, awaiting their final resurrection body; or, because of the nature of timeless eternity, they have received their resurrection bodies already because they live in the eternal "now."

iii. The truth that **to be absent from the body** means we will **be present with the Lord** proves two false doctrines to be false. It refutes the false doctrine of "soul sleep" (saying that the believing dead are held in some sort of suspended animation until the resurrection occurs) and the false doctrine of "purgatory" (saying that the believing dead must be "cleaned up" through their own suffering before coming into the presence of God).

iv. "He did not expect to be roasted alive for the next thousand years, and then to leap from purgatory to Paradise; but he did expect to go, as soon as ever his earthly house was dissolved, into his eternal house which is in the heavens. He had not even the thought of lying in a state of unconsciousness till the resurrection." (Spurgeon)

f. **To be present with the Lord**: This is what makes heaven really heaven, so we long **to be present with the Lord**. Heaven is precious to us for many reasons. We want to be with loved ones who have passed before us and whom we miss so dearly. We want to be with the great men and women of God who have passed before us in centuries past. We want to walk the streets of gold, see the pearly gates, and see the angels round the throne of God worshipping Him day and night. However, none of those things, precious as they are, make heaven really "heaven." What makes heaven really heaven is the unhindered, unrestricted presence of our Lord. The place of heaven would be like hell if we could not **be present with the Lord**.

4. (9-10) The aim of our life in light of our eternal destiny.

Therefore we make it our aim, whether present or absent, to be well pleasing to Him. For we must all appear before the judgment seat of Christ, that each one may receive the things *done* in the body, according to what he has done, whether good or bad.

a. **Therefore we make it our aim . . . to be well pleasing to Him**: Since what we do right now has eternal consequences, our goal must persistently be to please God.

i. "You report to headquarters. Never mind what anybody else thinks of you. Your business is to please Christ, and the less you trouble yourselves about pleasing men the more you will succeed in doing it." (Maclaren)

b. **Whether present or absent**: We can't do anything right now about pleasing God when we are absent from these bodies and present with the

2 Corinthians 5   61

Lord. That day has not yet come. Yet we can do something about pleasing the Lord when we are absent from His immediate presence and present in these bodies.

> i. We must consider that as far as we know, there are some opportunities for pleasing God that we will only have while **present** in these bodies. When we get to heaven, there will be no more need for faith, no more need for endurance through trials, no more need for courage and boldness in telling others about Jesus. *Now*, while we are **present** in these bodies, is our only opportunity in all eternity to please God in these areas.

c. **For we must all appear before the judgment seat of Christ**: When we pass from these bodies to the world beyond, we must each give account **according to what he has done, whether good or bad**.

> i. This is not the Great White Throne judgment (Revelation 20:11-15). This describes a judgment of the works of believers (**the things done in the body, according to what he has done, whether good or bad**).

> ii. The phrase **judgment seat** is a single word in the ancient Greek language of the New Testament. *Bema* literally means "step," as in a raised platform or seat. This was where a Roman magistrate sat to act as a judge. The *bema* was "an object of reverence and fear to all the people." (Hodge)

d. What will be judged at **the judgment seat of Christ**? First, *what we have done* will be judged (**the things done**). Secondly, our *motives* for what we have done will be judged (**according to what he has done, whether good or bad**).

> i. We must live understanding that *what we have done* will be judged. It is possible to have a saved soul and a wasted life, and that will be judged at the **judgment seat of Christ**. This should be an *encouragement* in our service to the Lord. It should remind us of the principle in Hebrews 6:10: *For God is not unjust to forget your work and labor of love which you have shown toward His name, in that you have ministered to the saints, and do minister.* Paul knows that the troubles of this life are worth it because he will be rewarded at the **judgment seat of Christ**.

> ii. We must live understanding that *our motives* for what we do will be judged (1 Corinthians 13:1-3 shares this idea). One can do the right things but with a wrong heart. God will often still use that person and even bring great blessing through them. Yet in the end, it is as if they did nothing for the Lord because their motives for service did not stand up at the **judgment seat of Christ**.

iii. Paul presents essentially the same idea in 1 Corinthians 3:12-15, where he speaks of a coming assessment of each one's work before the Lord. In that passage, he makes it clear that what we do and our motive for doing it will be tested by fire, and the purifying fire of God will burn up everything that was not of Him. We won't be *punished* for what was not done rightly unto the Lord; those things will simply be *burned up*, and it will be as if we never did them. We will simply be rewarded for what remains. Sadly, some will get to heaven *thinking* they have done great things for God and will find out at the **judgment seat of Christ** that they really did nothing.

iv. "Appearance before Christ's tribunal is the privilege of Christians. It is concerned with the assessment of works and, indirectly, of character, not with the determination of destiny; with reward, not status." (Harris)

5. (11) Our message in light of our eternal destiny.

Knowing, therefore, the terror of the Lord, we persuade men; but we are well known to God, and I also trust are well known in your consciences.

a. **Knowing, therefore, the terror of the Lord**: What do we know of the **terror of the Lord**? We know that apart from Jesus we are the righteous targets of **the terror of the Lord**. We also know that in Jesus we have been *delivered* from **the terror of the Lord**.

b. **We persuade men**: Knowing the place of men both apart from Jesus and the place of men in Jesus, **we persuade men** to come to Jesus and know what it means to be *delivered* from **the terror of the Lord**.

i. The message is not, "Watch out for **the terror of the Lord**," though there is a place for that message. The message is not, "If I don't persuade men I might face **the terror of the Lord**, so I better get to work!" Instead, the message is, "I have been delivered from **the terror of the Lord**, and you can be delivered too. Come to Jesus!" In truth, **the terror of the Lord** was targeted on *Jesus*, so it would not be directed at all those who trust in who Jesus is and what He has done for them.

ii. **We persuade men**: This should be the heart of everyone who presents the gospel, whether it is in a pulpit or anywhere else. We intend to **persuade men**. We are not simply casting out ideas without caring how men respond to them. We should be like Paul, who passionately desired that men and women come to Jesus. We must intend in our hearts and our words to **persuade men**.

c. **But we are well known to God, and I also trust are well known in your consciences**: Paul worked hard to **persuade men**, but he knew he did not need to persuade God. Instead, he knew that he was **well known to God**. He also wished that he did not need to persuade the Corinthian Christians; he wanted to **trust** that his message and his ministry were **well known in** their **consciences**.

> i. Paul saw the need to persuade *the world* of the person and work of Jesus and of his own integrity as a messenger of the good news. However, he knew there was no need to persuade God, and it frustrated him that it was necessary to persuade the Corinthian Christians.

B. Paul defends and describes his ministry.

1. (12) Why would Paul defend his ministry at all?

For we do not commend ourselves again to you, but give you opportunity to boast on our behalf, that you may have *an answer* for those who boast in appearance and not in heart.

a. **We do not commend ourselves again to you**: Was Paul just bragging? Was he just trying to glorify himself before the Corinthians? Not at all. Though Paul gloried in his weakness, his trials, and his struggles, he doesn't do it to brag before the Corinthian Christians.

b. **But give you opportunity to glory on our behalf**: Instead, by telling of his weakness, his trials, and his struggles, Paul wanted to give the Corinthian Christians the *opportunity* to be proud of him (**glory on our behalf**).

> i. Paul speaks with irony here. The Corinthian Christians were not interested in glorying in Paul or in seeing anything good in any of his trials. They thought the trials made Paul *less* of an apostle and man of God, not *more* of an apostle and man of God. Paul knew this well but is happy to give them the **opportunity to glory on our behalf** nonetheless!

c. **That you may have something to answer those who glory in appearance and not in heart**: One problem with the Corinthian Christians is that they *liked* **those who glory in appearance and not in heart**. They looked down on Paul because his glory was not **in appearance** and only **in heart**. By telling the Corinthian Christians how God worked through his struggles and trials, Paul gave them **something to answer those** who thought that way.

> i. What do you glory in? Are you among **those who glory in appearance and not in heart**? Remember what the Lord said to Samuel: *The LORD does not see as a man sees; for man looks at the outward appearance, but*

the LORD *looks at the heart* (1 Samuel 16:7). We are so easily impressed by a person's *image* that we often do not see or care about their *substance*. It isn't that **appearance** is completely unimportant, but compared to the **heart** it almost is.

2. (13-15) Paul isn't crazy; instead, he is motivated by the love of God he has received.

For if we are beside ourselves, *it is* for God; or if we are of sound mind, *it is* for you. For the love of Christ compels us, because we judge thus: that if One died for all, then all died; and He died for all, that those who live should live no longer for themselves, but for Him who died for them and rose again.

a. **If we are beside ourselves**: To be "beside yourself" describes crazy, irrational behavior. The Corinthian Christians probably thought Paul was crazy because he seemed content with a life of pain, trials, and discomfort if it brought glory to God. In being accused of being beside himself, Paul is in good company. Jesus was also accused of being out of His mind (Mark 3:21 and John 10:20).

i. "Probably he was reputed by some to be *deranged*. Festus thought so: *Paul, thou art beside thyself; too much learning hath made thee mad.* And his enemies at Corinth might insinuate not only that he was *deranged*, but attribute his derangement to a less worthy cause than intense study and deep learning." (Clarke)

b. **If we are beside ourselves, it is for God; or if we are of sound mind, it is for you**: Paul doesn't want the Corinthian Christians to think he is *deliberately* acting in a way that some might think crazy, just for the sake of acting crazy. Instead, he is doing it **for God**. Then again, if the Corinthian Christians want to think Paul is **of sound mind**, they can think he is acting that way for them.

i. "The apostle tells them, that if indeed he was beside himself in any of their opinion, it was *to God*, that is, for the honour and glory of God: or if he was sober, it was for their sake; in what temper so ever he was, it was either for service to God, or them." (Poole)

c. **For the love of Christ constrains us**: Paul is motivated - even pushed on by - the **love of Christ**, that is, Jesus' love towards him. Paul *had* to do what he did in ministry, because he received so much love from Jesus that it compelled him to serve others.

i. This is the greatest foundation for ministry, wanting to give *something* to others because Jesus gave you *everything*. When we really receive the **love of Christ**, it touches us and makes us want to serve others.

ii. Paul felt *compelled* by **the love of Christ**. If someone asked, "Why are you doing it all? Why all the pain and all the trials?" Paul would answer, "I have to. I have received **the love of Christ**. I have **the love of Christ** in my heart in the sense that I love Jesus. I also have **the love of Christ** in my heart for all the people Jesus loves. I am compelled by **the love of Christ!**" "The apostles laboured much, but all their labour sprang from the impulse of the love of Jesus Christ. Just as Jacob toiled for Rachel solely out of love to her, so do true saints serve the Lord Jesus under the omnipotent constraint of love." (Spurgeon)

iii. To say, "**the love of Christ constrains us,**" is to say that the love of Christ has *power*. It has a force that can bind us and influence us. "The love of Christ had pressed Paul's energies into one force, turned them into one channel, and then driven them forward with a wonderful force, till he and his fellows had become a mighty power for good, ever active and energetic." (Spurgeon)

d. **If one died for all, then all died**: How did Jesus **die for all**? In the sense that His death is *able* to save **all** who will come to Him and is a *demonstration* of God's love to **all**; but *not* in the sense that all are saved because Jesus died (which is the false doctrine of universalism).

i. However, it is probable that in this context Paul means "all the saved" when he says **all**. There is no doubt that there is a sense in which Jesus died for the whole world: *And He Himself is the propitiation for our sins, and not for ours only but also for the whole world* (1 John 2:2). But the **all** Paul mentions here is probably "all the saved," because he also writes **then all died**. It can only be said that those who join themselves to Jesus by faith have spiritually died and risen again with Him (Romans 6:1-6).

e. **That those who live should live no longer for themselves, but for Him who died for them and rose again**: If Jesus died for us, it is only fitting that we live **for Him**. Jesus gave us new life, not to live for ourselves but to live **for Him**. The question is simple: Are you living for yourself, or are you living for Jesus? "He died for us that we might die to ourselves." (Calvin)

i. God created us for the purpose of living for Him, not for ourselves. It is a corruption of our nature that makes us want to live for ourselves and not for the Lord. In Revelation 4:11 it says in the King James Version: *for thou hast created all things, and for thy pleasure they are and were created*. We *are and were created* to live unto God, not unto ourselves. Jesus lived *completely* unto God the Father.

ii. What does it mean to **live no longer for themselves, but for Him?** It doesn't mean that we can say, "I won't love or serve anyone else but God." Instead, our love for God, and our life for God, is expressed in the way we serve others. When we say that we live for God, we can not use it as an excuse to neglect serving others.

3. (16) Because of this new life made possible by Jesus, old earthly attachments are far less important.

Therefore, from now on, we regard no one according to the flesh. Even though we have known Christ according to the flesh, yet now we know *Him thus* no longer.

a. **We regard no one according to the flesh:** Why?

- Because we *do not look at the things which are seen, but at the things which are not seen* (2 Corinthians 4:18)

- Because our *earthly tent* will be destroyed, but we will have a new body, *eternal in the heavens* (2 Corinthians 5:1)

- Because *we walk by faith, not by sight* (2 Corinthians 5:7)

- Because we do not *glory in appearance*, but we glory *in heart* (2 Corinthians 5:12)

i. For all these reasons, we don't look to the image and appearance of the flesh but to the substance of the heart.

b. **Even though we have known Christ according to the flesh, yet we know Him thus no longer:** Even those who knew Jesus in the flesh found their new relationship with Him through the Holy Spirit far more rewarding.

i. Because Paul writes **we have known Christ according to the flesh**, we can surmise that Paul knew of Jesus during the days of His earthly ministry and probably even heard Jesus teach in Jerusalem. Paul may have even been among some of the Pharisees who often confronted Jesus! Paul certainly fondly looked back on what he remembered of **Christ according to the flesh**. At the same time, he knew his relationship with Jesus through the Holy Spirit was far better.

ii. "When he knew Christ after the flesh he considered Him as the leader of a new sect, the leader of a new party, a menace to holy religion. He says we do not see Him like that any more. We know Him now in the Spirit, by the Spirit." (Morgan)

iii. So, to have known Jesus in the flesh didn't guarantee anything. "Great numbers had followed Christ in person who afterwards deserted Him and demanded His crucifixion." (Hughes) Even the disciples were poor followers of Jesus until they knew Him by the Spirit on the day of Pentecost.

c. **We know Him thus no longer:** Some think that it would be better if Jesus were present with us **according to the flesh**, but it would not be and Jesus knew this. This is why Jesus told His disciples *It is to your advantage that I go away; for if I do not go away, the Helper will not come to you; but if I depart, I will send Him to you* (John 16:7).

4. (17) The resurrection life of Jesus gives us new life.

Therefore, if anyone *is* in Christ, *he is* a new creation; old things have passed away; behold, all things have become new.

a. **If anyone:** This is a promise for **anyone. Anyone!** It doesn't matter what class, what race, what nationality, what language, or what level of intelligence. **Anyone** can be a new creation in Jesus Christ.

b. **Is in Christ:** This is a promise for **anyone** who **is in Christ**. This is not a promise for those who are in themselves, or in the religion of men, or in someone or something else. This is for those **in Christ**.

c. **He is a new creation; old things have passed away; behold, all things have become new.** Paul here teaches the great principle of *regeneration*. Jesus Christ changes those who come to Him by faith and who are **in Christ**. The saved are not *"just* forgiven." They are changed into a **new creation**.

i. It is unfair for us to expect those who are not **in Christ** to live as if they were **a new creation**. However, it is *not* unfair to expect a changed life from people who say they are Christians. "I know no language, I believe there is none, that can express a greater or more thorough and more radical renewal, than that which is expressed in the term, 'a new creature.' " (Spurgeon)

ii. However, being a **new creation** doesn't mean that we are perfect. It means that we *are* changed and that we are *being* changed.

d. Who makes us **a new creation?** This is something God alone can do in us. This isn't just "turning over a new leaf" or "getting your act together." Yet the life of a **new creation** is not something God does *for us* but *in us*. So, we are told to *put off . . . the old man* and to *put on the new man which was created according to God, in righteousness and true holiness* (Ephesians 4:22-24).

i. Being **a new creation** is a gift from God received by faith. "God is surely the author of the second creation as he was of the first." (Harris) "A phrase which argueth the greatest change imaginable, and such a one as can be wrought in the soul by no other power than the power of God." (Poole)

ii. The work of **a new creation** is even greater than God's work of creating the world. "My brethren, it was more difficult, if such terms are ever applicable to Omnipotence, it was more difficult to create a Christian than to create a world. What was there to begin with when God made the world? There was nothing; but nothing could not stand in God's way - it was at least passive. But, my brethren, in our hearts, while there was nothing that could help God, there was much that could and did oppose him. Our stubborn wills, our deep prejudices, our ingrained love of iniquity, all these, great God, opposed thee, and aimed at thwarting thy designs . . . Yes, great God, it was great to make a world, but greater to create a new creature in Jesus Christ." (Spurgeon)

iii. Living as **a new creation** is something God works in us, using our will and our choices. So, we must both *receive the gift* of being **a new creation** and be challenged to *live the life* of **a new creation**. All this is God's work in us that we must submit to. This reminds us that at its root, Christianity is all about what *God did for us*, not what we can or should *do for God*. "Beloved, if you have no more religion than you have worked out in yourself, and no more grace than you have found in your nature, you have none at all. A supernatural work of the Holy Ghost must be wrought in every one of us, if we would see the face of God with acceptance." (Spurgeon)

e. **All things have become new** is the language of God's perfect, recreated work (Revelation 21:5). God wants to do a **new** thing in our life.

i. "The man is not only *mended*, but he is *new made* . . . there is a *new creation*, which God himself owns as his workmanship, and which he can look on and pronounce *very good*." (Clarke)

5. (18-19) The message and ministry of reconciliation.

Now all things *are* of God, who has reconciled us to Himself through Jesus Christ, and has given us the ministry of reconciliation, that is, that God was in Christ reconciling the world to Himself, not imputing their trespasses to them, and has committed to us the word of reconciliation.

a. **All things are of God**: Paul soars high here and wants the Corinthian Christians to know that he is writing of things that **are of God**, not of man. This work of *a new creation* and our eternal destiny are works **of God**, not something we have to earn and achieve.

b. **God, who has reconciled us to Himself through Jesus Christ**: God initiated this ministry of reconciliation, even though He is the innocent party in the estranged relationship. He **reconciled us to Himself**; we did not reconcile ourselves to Him.

i. Importantly, God did this **through Jesus Christ**. God did not **reconcile us to Himself** by neglecting His holy justice, or "giving in" to sinful, rebellious humanity. He did it by an amazing, righteous, sacrifice of love. God demands not one bit less justice and righteousness from man under Jesus, but the demand has been satisfied **through Jesus Christ**.

c. **And has given us the ministry of reconciliation**: Having **has reconciled us to Himself through Jesus Christ**, now God expects us to take up the **ministry of reconciliation** and has therefore **committed to us the word of reconciliation**.

i. Reconciliation comes by **the word of reconciliation**. God uses the preached word to reconcile men and women to Himself.

d. **God was in Christ reconciling the world to Himself**: Through all the terrors of the cross, God the Father worked in and with God the Son, **reconciling the world to Himself**. The Father and the Son worked *together* on the cross.

i. **God was in Christ reconciling the world to Himself** is all the more amazing when understood in light of what happened on the cross. At some point before Jesus died, before the veil was torn in two, before Jesus cried out *"it is finished,"* an awesome spiritual transaction took place. The Father set upon the Son all the guilt and wrath our sin deserved, and Jesus bore it in Himself perfectly, totally satisfying the justice of God for us.

ii. As horrible as the physical suffering of Jesus was, this spiritual suffering - the act of being judged for sin in our place - was what Jesus really dreaded about the cross. This was the *cup* - the cup of God's righteous wrath - that He trembled at drinking (Luke 22:39-46, Psalm 75:8, Isaiah 51:17, Jeremiah 25:15). On the cross Jesus became, as it were, an enemy of God who was judged and forced to drink the cup of the Father's fury so that we would not have to drink that cup.

iii. Yet, at the same time, Paul makes it clear that **God was in Christ reconciling the world to Himself**. They worked together. Though Jesus was being *treated* as if He were an enemy of God, He was not. Even as Jesus was punished as if He were a sinner, He performed the most holy service unto God the Father ever offered. This is why Isaiah can say, *Yet it pleased the* LORD *to bruise Him* (Isaiah 53:10). In and of itself, the suffering of the Son did not please the Father, but as it accomplished the work of **reconciling the world to Himself**, it completely pleased God the Father.

iv. Robertson rightly comments: "We may not dare to probe too far into this mystery of Christ's suffering on the Cross, but this fact throws some light on the tragic cry of Jesus just before he died: 'My God, My God, why didst thou forsake me?' " In that cry (Matthew 27:46 and Mark 15:34), Jesus expresses both His partnership with God the Father (*My God*) and the agonizing feeling of receiving the wrath of God that we deserved.

e. **Not imputing their trespasses to them**: Why? Was it because God went soft and gave mankind a "Get Out of Hell Free" card? Not at all. Instead, it is because our trespasses *were* imputed to Jesus. The justice our sin demanded is satisfied, not excused.

i. If God sets aside His wrath or His justice to save sinners, then the cross, instead of being a demonstration of love, is an exhibition of unspeakable cruelty and injustice, and of one man's misguided attempt at do-goodism. If sin could just be *excused*, then it never needed to be *satisfied*.

6. (20) Ambassadors for Christ.

Now then, we are ambassadors for Christ, as though God were pleading through us: we implore *you* on Christ's behalf, be reconciled to God.

a. **Therefore we are ambassadors for Christ**: Paul sees that he serves in a foreign land as the representative of a King. The King has a message, and Paul is delivering that message **as though God were pleading through us**.

i. There is so much to the idea of being **ambassadors**! An ambassador does not speak to please his audience, but the King who sent him. An ambassador does not speak on his own authority; his own opinions or demands mean little. He simply says what he has been commissioned to say. But an ambassador is more than a messenger; he is also a representative, and the honor and reputation of his country are in his hands.

b. **Ambassadors**: This is a glorious title for Paul and the other apostles. However, it is not more glorious or more stunning than the thought of God, out of love, **pleading** to man. Why should God plead for us?

c. **We implore you on Christ's behalf, be reconciled to God**: As an ambassador Paul makes a simple, strong, direct plea: **be reconciled to God**.

i. This makes it clear that the work of reconciliation mentioned previously in the chapter does not work apart from our will and our choice.

Who are the ones **reconciled to God**? Those who have responded to Jesus' plea, made through His ambassadors.

ii. This makes it clear that it is *we* who must be **reconciled to God**, not He to us. *We* are the party in the wrong.

iii. Who is Paul imploring? The **you** of **we implore you** was added by the translators. Paul may have said, "*We implore the whole world on Christ's behalf*," or he may have said, "*We implore you Corinthian Christians on Christ's behalf*." The thought is valid either way, and both ideas may be in mind.

d. **Be reconciled**: We are not commanded to do the work of reconciliation between man and God. He has done the work; it is merely ours to embrace and receive. "It is not so much reconcile yourselves as 'be reconciled.' Yield yourselves to him who round you now the bands of a man would cast, drawing you with cords of love because he was given for you . . . Submit yourselves. Yield to the grasp of those hands which were nailed to the cross for you." (Spurgeon)

7. (21) How God made reconciliation possible.

For He made Him who knew no sin *to be* sin for us, that we might become the righteousness of God in Him.

a. **Him who knew no sin**: The idea that any man could be sinless was foreign to Jewish thinking (Ecclesiastes 8:5). Despite that, no one challenged Jesus when He claimed to be sinless (John 8:46).

b. **He made Him who knew no sin to be sin for us**: Under the inspiration of the Holy Spirit, Paul carefully chooses his words. He does not say Jesus was made *to be a sinner.* Jesus never became a *sinner*, but He did become **sin for us**. Even His becoming sin was a righteous act of love, not an act of sin.

i. Jesus was not a sinner, even on the cross. On the cross, the Father treated Him as if He were a sinner, yet all the while, sin was "outside" of Jesus not "inside" Him and it was not a part of His nature (as it is with us).

ii. "Christ was not guilty, and could not be made guilty; but he was treated as if he were guilty, because he willed to stand in the place of the guilty. Yea, he was not only treated as a sinner, but he was treated as if he had been sin itself in the abstract. This is an amazing utterance. The sinless one was made to be sin." (Spurgeon)

iii. "I do not say that our substitute endured a hell, that were unwarrantable. I will not say that he endured either the exact punishment for sin, or an equivalent for it; but I do say that what he endured rendered to the justice of God a vindication of his law more clear and more effectual than would have been rendered to it by the damnation of sinners for whom he died." (Spurgeon)

iv. "We obviously stand at the brink of a great mystery and our understanding of it can only be minimal." (Kruse)

c. Note well that **He made Him**. This is the work of God Himself! The Father and the Son (and the Spirit as well) were in perfect cooperation in the work on the cross. This means that the work of atonement on the cross was *the work of God.* "If God did it, it is well done. I am not careful to defend an act of God: let the man who dares accuse his Maker think what he is at. If God himself provided the sacrifice, be you sure that he has accepted it." (Spurgeon)

d. **That we might become the righteousness of God in Him**: Jesus *took* our sin, but *gave* us His **righteousness**. It is a tremendous exchange, all prompted by the love of God for us!

i. "Not only does the believer receive from God a right standing before him on the basis of faith in Jesus (Phil 3:9), but here Paul says that 'in Christ' the believer in some sense actually shares the righteousness that characterizes God himself." (Harris)

ii. **The righteousness of God**: "What a grand expression! He makes us righteous through the righteousness of Jesus; nay, not only makes us righteous, but *righteousness;* nay, that is not all, he makes us the righteousness *of God;* that is higher than the righteousness of Adam in the garden, it is more divinely perfect than angelic perfection." (Spurgeon)

iii. "The righteousness which Adam had in the garden was perfect, but it was the righteousness of man: ours is the righteousness of God." (Spurgeon)

iv. This is the whole truth of justification stated simply: Our sins were on Jesus, and His righteousness is on us. And, "As Christ was not made sin by any sin inherent in him, so neither are we made righteous by any righteousness inherent in us, but by the righteousness of Christ imputed to us." (Poole)

2 Corinthians 6 - Paul's Resume'

A. The seriousness and character of Paul's ministry.

1. (1-2) The responsibility of God's great offer.

We then, *as* workers together *with Him* also plead with *you* not to receive the grace of God in vain. For He says: "In an acceptable time I have heard you, and in the day of salvation I have helped you." Behold, now *is* the accepted time; behold, now *is* the day of salvation.

a. **Workers together with Him**: Paul sees himself as a co-worker with Jesus Christ. They are partners, and Jesus *has given us the ministry of reconciliation* (2 Corinthians 5:18). Since Paul is among the *ambassadors for Christ* (2 Corinthians 5:20), he works with Jesus.

i. What an amazing job: **workers together with Him**! It isn't that God *needed* Paul, or any of us. Instead, it is that God wants us to be **workers together with Him** for *our* good. It's like the little boy with the toy lawnmower following dad as dad mows the lawn. For the sake of pure efficiency, dad should ask the boy to go away because he is really just in the way. But it is so good for the boy to work with dad! And because dad loves his boy, he wants him to work **together with Him**.

ii. The word "**workers**" itself is important. There is something good and important in work itself, so much so that God wants us to be **workers together with Him**. God's best for our life is never a state of ease and comfort and indulgent inactivity - even if we did all those things **together with Him**. God wants us to be **workers together with Him**, not "couch potatoes" or "pew potatoes" together with Him.

iii. We are **workers together with Him**. Paul never said God *works together with* us. It isn't *our work* that God helps us with. It is *His work* that He asks us to do **together with Him**. Instead of trying to get

God to help us with our work, we need to find out what God's work is, and do it **with Him**.

iv. The picture of *ambassadors for Christ* (2 Corinthians 5:20) is especially helpful in understanding the nature of being **workers together with Him**. An ambassador can rightly be described as working together with his king. Yet, the ambassador himself has no power or authority or agenda on his own - it is all bound up in his king. The king *delegates* power and authority to the ambassador and reveals his agenda to the ambassador, and then the king expects the ambassador to fulfill that agenda.

b. **Also plead with you**: Paul told us that God was *pleading* through the ministry of the apostles (2 Corinthians 5:20). Now Paul will **also plead with** the Corinthian Christians. To **plead** is to beg, and Paul isn't too proud to beg with eternity on the line.

c. **Not to receive the grace of God in vain**: The Corinthian Christians had obviously received **the grace of God**. They would not be Christians at all had they not received **the grace of God**. Yet having received it, they were potentially guilty of receiving **the grace of God in vain**, so Paul pleads with them to *not* do this.

i. What does it mean to **receive the grace of God in vain**? It means to receive the goodness and favor of God, yet to hinder the work of grace in one's life. It means to receive the favor of God and to fail in what Paul spoke of in 1 Corinthians 15:10: *But by the grace of God I am what I am, and His grace toward me was not in vain; but I labored more abundantly than they all, yet not I, but the grace of God which was with me.*

ii. According to 1 Corinthians 15:10, if Paul did not work as hard as he did, the grace of God would still be given to him, but in some measure it would have been given **in vain**. Grace, by definition, is given freely, but how we receive grace will help to determine how effective the gift of grace is. *Grace* is "frequently used by St. Paul to express the favours and privileges offered to the members of the Church of Christ, not to be limited to grace given at any special moment (such as at salvation) . . . it is offered, independently of man's faith and obedience, but it will not profit without these." (Bernard)

iii. Grace isn't given because of any works, past, present or promised; yet it is given to *encourage* work, not to say work is unnecessary. God doesn't want us to receive His grace and become passive. Paul knew that God gives His grace, we work hard, and the work of God is done.

iv. Many Christians struggle at this very point. Is God supposed to do it or am I supposed to do it? The answer is, "Yes!" God does it and we do it. Trust God, rely on Him, *and then get to work and work as hard as you can!* That is how we see the work of God accomplished. If I neglect my end of the partnership, God's grace doesn't accomplish all that it might and is therefore given **in vain**.

v. "God's grace is always coming to my heart and life in very wonderful and blessed experience of now. Yesterday's grace is totally inadequate for the burden of today, and if I do not learn to lay hold of heavenly resources every day of my life for the little things as well as the big things, as a Christian I soon become stale, barren, and fruitless in the service of the Lord." (Redpath)

d. **Now is the acceptable time . . . now is the day of salvation**: By quoting and applying Isaiah 49:8, Paul wants to give the Corinthian Christians a sense of urgency. God has an **acceptable time** for us to work with His grace. God has a **day of salvation** that will not last forever. This is no time for Christian lives consumed with ease and comfort and self-focus. It is time to get busy for the Lord and to be **workers together with Him**.

2. (3) How this responsibility affected Paul: his passion to be blameless as a servant of the gospel.

We give no offense in anything, that our ministry may not be blamed.

a. **We give no offense in anything**: Paul was willing to do most anything to make sure he gave **no offense in anything**. He was willing to forego his salary as a minister of the gospel (1 Corinthians 9:3-15). He was willing to allow others to be more prominent. He was willing to work hard and endure hardship. Paul was not afraid to offend anyone over the gospel of Jesus Christ (1 Corinthians 1:18-25), but he would not allow his style of ministry to offend anyone.

b. **That our ministry may not be blamed**: Of course, Paul's ministry *was* blamed and discredited by the Corinthian Christians. What Paul means is **that our ministry may not** *rightly* **be blamed**. Paul could not do anything about false accusations except live in such a way that any fair-minded person would see such accusations as false.

3. (4-10) Paul's credentials as a blameless minister.

But in all *things* we commend ourselves as ministers of God: in much patience, in tribulations, in needs, in distresses, in stripes, in imprisonments, in tumults, in labors, in sleeplessness, in fastings; by purity, by knowledge, by longsuffering, by kindness, by the Holy Spirit, by sincere love, by the word of truth, by the power of God, by the armor of righteousness on the right hand and on the left, by honor and dishonor, by evil report and good report; as deceivers, and *yet* true; as unknown,

and *yet* well known; as dying, and behold we live; as chastened, and *yet* not killed; as sorrowful, yet always rejoicing; as poor, yet making many rich; as having nothing, and *yet* possessing all things.

a. **In all things we commend ourselves**: Paul will now recount his resume' to the Corinthian Christians. Here are the things he will list to **commend** himself before them.

b. **In much patience**: Paul's first qualification was **patience**. The ancient Greek word used here is *hupomone*, which has the idea of *endurance* instead of simply "waiting."

i. We often think of **patience** as a passive thing - the ability to sit around and wait for something to happen. That is not the idea of the word Paul used here. It is an *active endurance* instead of a *passive waiting*. The ancient Greek word *hupomone* "does not describe the frame of mind which can sit down with folded hands and bowed head and let a torrent of troubles sweep over it in passive resignation. It describes the ability to bear things in such a triumphant way that it transfigures them." (Barclay)

c. **Tribulations, needs** and **distresses**: In Paul's resume' as an apostle, ambassador, and co-worker with Jesus, he follows **patience** with describing *why* he needed this endurance. First, it was because of the *general struggles and trials of life*. Paul was often stressed and under pressure (this is the idea behind the word for **tribulations**), often needy, and often in distress.

i. "*Distresses* signify, properly, a man's being straitened, or thrust up in a place, so as that he knoweth not how to steer himself; and, metaphorically, a want of counsel, not knowing what to do, or which way to turn ourselves." (Poole)

d. **Stripes, imprisonments**, and **tumults**: As Paul continues his resume', he writes of *sufferings directly inflicted by men*. **Stripes** were the wounds on the back from a whipping, **imprisonments** referred to the frequent time Paul spent in jail, and **tumults** speak of violence from an angry mob.

i. "Nowadays it is not the violence but the mockery or the amused contempt of the crowd against which the Christian must stand fast." (Barclay)

e. **Labors, sleeplessness**, and **fastings**: Paul continues his resume' with describing *his self-inflicted hardships*. No one made him work so hard, keep so many sleepless nights, or go without food so often. These were true trials but ones Paul chose willingly as a co-worker with Jesus Christ. Paul isn't complaining about these, because they were self-inflicted, but they were relevant to his need for patience.

i. Paul knew he needed endurance, and he knew many things in his life drew him to seek that endurance. Some of them were the general trials of life, some were sufferings directly brought by others, and some were self-inflicted. Not every trial was the same, but they all made him need endurance.

f. **By purity, by knowledge, by longsuffering, by kindness, by the Holy Spirit, by sincere love, by the word of truth, by the power of God, by the armor of righteousness on the right hand and on the left**: Here, Paul begins to describe the resources he took advantage of in triumphing over adversity. If he honestly listed his trials, he will also honestly list the fruit of the Spirit and the power of God in his life.

i. Yes, Paul had the trials of 2 Corinthians 6:4-5 in greater measure than most men. Yet he also had the blessings of 2 Corinthians 6:6-7 in greater measure than most men.

ii. The idea of **on the right hand and on the left** is of holding both offensive and defensive weapons. It probably has in mind "both advancing and being attacked." "Particularly, the *shield* and the *sword*; the former on the *left arm*, the latter on the *right hand*. We have the doctrine of truth, and the power of God, as an armour to protect us on *all sides*, *every where*, and *on all occasions*." (Clarke)

g. **By honor and dishonor, by evil report and good report; as deceivers, and yet true; as unknown, and yet well known; as dying, and behold we live; as chastened, and yet not killed; as sorrowful, yet always rejoicing; as poor, yet making many rich; as having nothing, and yet possessing all things**. In concluding his resume', Paul will list his references, describing both what the world thought of him and what God thought of him.

i. The world (including the worldly Corinthian Christians) described Paul with words like: **dishonor . . . evil report . . . deceivers . . . unknown . . . dying . . . chastened . . . sorrowful . . . poor . . . having nothing**.

ii. In His reference, God described Paul with words like: **honor . . . good report . . . true . . . well known . . . behold we live . . . not killed . . . always rejoicing . . . making many rich . . . possessing all things**.

iii. Which description was true - the world's or God's? 2 Corinthians 4:18 gives the answer. According to *the things which are seen*, the world's estimation was correct. According to the *things which are not seen*, God's estimation was correct. Which estimation is more important to you?

B. Paul speaks to the Corinthians as a father.

1. (11-13) Paul's desire for reconciliation.

O Corinthians! We have spoken openly to you, our heart is wide open. You are not restricted by us, but you are restricted by your *own* affections. Now in return for the same (I speak as to children), you also be open.

a. **O Corinthians!** Paul has spent enough time laying down the principles. Now he makes a pointed appeal to the Corinthian Christians. We can sense the depth and passion in his heart as he cries "**O Corinthians!**"

b. **We have spoken openly to you, our heart is wide open:** Paul is practicing what he preached in Ephesians 4:15: *speaking the truth in love.* He genuinely loved the Corinthians with an open heart, yet he would also speak openly to them.

c. **You are not restricted by us, but you are restricted by your own affections:** The Corinthian Christians played the "victim" before Paul. Out of godly necessity he was firm with them on previous occasions (1 Corinthians 4:18-21, 2 Corinthians 1:23). Now, they probably claimed to be **restricted** by the "hurt" Paul caused them. They probably said, "We would love to reconcile with you Paul, but the pain you caused us restricts us. We just can't get over it."

i. But the real problem was that the Corinthian Christians were **restricted by** [their] **own affections**. It wasn't that *Paul* did not love them enough (which was their claim as "victims"). It was that *they* loved too much! Their own affections **restricted** them.

ii. What did they love too much? First, they loved the world too much, and Paul will deal with that love in following verses. They also loved *themselves* too much and refused to really deal with their selfish and worldly attitudes towards Paul.

d. **You also be open:** Paul wants to see the same self-searching honesty in the Corinthian Christians that he just displayed to them. They had to do this so that they could be reconciled. The rift between Paul and the Corinthian church could be healed, but it was in the hands of the Corinthian Christians to do it. They had to **also be open**.

2. (14-18) Paul tells them to narrow their love.

Do not be unequally yoked together with unbelievers. For what fellowship has righteousness with lawlessness? And what communion has light with darkness? And what accord has Christ with Belial? Or what part has a believer with an unbeliever? And what agreement has the temple of God with idols? For you are the temple of the living God. As God has said: "I will dwell in them and walk among *them*. I will be their God,

and they shall be My people." Therefore "Come out from among them and be separate, says the Lord. Do not touch what is unclean, and I will receive you. I will be a Father to you, and you shall be My sons and daughters, says the Lord Almighty."

a. **Do not be unequally yoked together with unbelievers:** Paul is speaking to the overly broad affections of the Corinthian Christians. They had joined themselves to **unbelievers,** and this prevented their reconciliation with Paul.

> i. The idea of **do not be unequally yoked together** is based on Deuteronomy 22:9, which prohibited yoking together two different animals. It speaks of joining two things that should not be joined.

> ii. In what ways had the Corinthian Christians become **unequally yoked together with unbelievers?** How can we do this? Certainly by marrying an unbeliever, which is the most common way this principle is applied. "A very wise and very holy man was given his judgment on this point: 'A man who is truly pious, marrying with an unconverted woman, will either draw back to perdition, or have a cross during life.' The same may be said of a *pious woman* marrying an *unconverted man.* Such persons cannot say this petition of the Lord's prayer, *Lead us not into temptation.* They *plunge* into it of their own accord." (Clarke)

> iii. However, Paul means much more here than only marrying an unbeliever. It really applies to any environment where we let the world influence our thinking. When we are being *conformed to this world* and are not being *transformed by the renewing of your mind* (Romans 12:2), we join together with unbelievers in an ungodly way.

> iv. This speaks especially to the issue of *influence.* Paul is not suggesting that Christians never associate with unbelievers (he makes this clear in 1 Corinthians 5:9-13). The principle is that we are to be *in* the world, but not *of* the world, like a ship should be in the water, but water shouldn't be in the ship. If the world is *influencing* us, it is clear we are **unequally yoked together with unbelievers.** And this unequal yoke, or ungodly influence, may come through a book, a movie, a television show, a magazine, or even through worldly Christian friends. Most Christians are *far too indiscriminate* about the things they allow to influence their minds and lives.

> v. We all like to believe that we can be around ungodly things as much as we want and that we are strong enough to ward off the influence. But we must take seriously the words of Scripture: *Do not be deceived: "Evil company corrupts good habits"* (1 Corinthians 15:33). It needs to come back to the simple question from Romans 12:2: Are we being

conformed to this world, or are we being *transformed by the renewing of your mind?*

vi. The Corinthian Christians thought like worldly people, not like godly people. They gained this way of looking at life - or at least they stayed in it - because of their ungodly associations. Paul tells them to break those yokes of fellowship with the ungodly!

b. **What fellowship has righteousness with lawlessness?** The Corinthian Christians were too loving and too affectionate in the sense that they thought it was "accepting" of them to allow **lawlessness** with **righteousness**, to accept **darkness** along with the **light**, and to admit **Belial** along with **Christ**.

i. **Belial** is a word borrowed from Hebrew, meaning *worthlessness* or *wickedness*. Here it is used as another word for *Satan*. "The term is used only in this place in the New Testament, but very often in the Old Testament, to express men notoriously wicked and scandalous." (Poole)

c. **What communion has light with darkness?** By using the term **communion**, Paul indicates that he really means *influence* more than *presence*. "Parties are said to be in communion when they are so united that what belongs to the one belongs to the other, or when what is true of the one is true of the other." (Hodge)

d. **What agreement has the temple of God with idols?** Apparently, the Corinthian Christians still struggled with the idolatry problem Paul referred to in 1 Corinthians 8-10. Their association with **idols** influenced their thinking, making it more and more worldly.

e. **You are the temple of the living God**: In 1 Corinthians 6:19-20, Paul wrote of individual Christians as being temples of God. Here, he refers to the church as a whole being the temple. Because temples are holy places and should be protected against things that might defile the holy place, we should protect our hearts and minds as holy places before the Lord.

i. So, because Ezekiel 37:26-27 tells us God is in the midst of His temple (**I will dwell in them and walk among them**), Isaiah 52:11 tells us how we should make that temple a holy place (**Come out from among them and be separate . . . do not touch what is unclean**). The promise **and I will receive you** reminds us that this is not only a separation *from* evil but also a separation *unto* God. "It is not a question simply of trying to empty your heart and life of every worldly desire - what an awful impossibility! It is rather opening your heart wide to all the love of God in Christ, and letting that love just sweep through you and exercise its expulsive power till your heart is filled with love." (Redpath)

ii. Paul quotes Jeremiah 31:9 to show the benefit of separating from worldly influence: a more intimate relationship with God (**I will be a Father to you, and you shall be My sons and daughters**). There is always a glorious promise for those who are willing to separate themselves from the world's influences for the sake of godliness.

iii. As Paul quotes these passages, he isn't necessarily quoting them word-for-word from either the Hebrew or the Septuagint. When Paul quotes Scripture, he often paraphrases it. "A comparison of texts reveals that he did not feel himself bound to quote slavishly word for word, but rather according to the sense and with the purpose of applying and showing the relevance of the revelation to the circumstances of his readers." (Hughes)

f. **Come out from among them and be separate**: This call deals with the problem of "too much affection" Paul mentioned in 2 Corinthians 6:12. We really can love too much, thinking we may just *add* the love of God without renouncing the ideas of Satan and this world. Remember that one of the seeds that failed in the parable of the soils had ground that was *too* fertile. It would grow *everything*.

g. **Says the LORD Almighty**: The title **Almighty** uses the ancient Greek word *pantokrater*, which means, "the one who has his hand on everything." In the whole New Testament, the word is used only here and in the book of Revelation. Paul wants us to understand that it is the sovereign God of heaven who offers us adoption as His children as we separate unto Him.

i. The call to purity and separation unto God flows from the offer of reconciliation mentioned at the end of 2 Corinthians 5. "A man cannot accept reconciliation with God and live in sin; because the renunciation of sin is involved in the acceptance of reconciliation. Paul never assumes that men may accept one benefit of redemption, and reject another. They cannot take pardon and refuse sanctification." (Hodge)

2 Corinthians 7 - Comforted by the Corinthian Christians' Repentance

A. Cleansing and perfecting.

1. (1a) In light of God's promises.

Therefore, having these promises.

a. **Therefore, having these promises**: This is Paul's natural conclusion to 2 Corinthians 6:14-18. In that passage, Paul wrote about the need to separate from worldly influences so that we can live a close life with God.

b. The commandment to *come out from among them and be separate* (2 Corinthians 6:17) is coupled with a promise: *I will receive you. I will be a Father to you, and you shall be My sons and daughters* (2 Corinthians 6:18). If we separate ourselves from worldly thinking and acting, we are promised a closer relationship with God.

2. (1b) Two things to do in light of God's promises.

Beloved, let us cleanse ourselves from all filthiness of the flesh and spirit, perfecting holiness in the fear of God.

a. **Cleanse ourselves from all filthiness**: This is what we *take away*. There is a cleansing that God alone does in our lives, but there is also a cleansing that God wants to do in cooperation with us. Here, Paul writes about a cleansing that isn't just something God does for us as we sit passively; this is a self-cleansing for intimacy with God that goes beyond a general cleansing for sin.

i. There is a main aspect of cleansing that comes to us as we trust in Jesus and His work on our behalf. This work of cleansing is really God's work in us and not our work. This is the sense of 1 John 1:9: *If we confess our sins, He is faithful and just to forgive us our sins and to cleanse us from all unrighteousness.*

ii. But there is another aspect of cleansing that God looks for us to do with the participation of our own will and effort; not that it is our work apart from God, but it is a work that awaits our will and effort: **let us cleanse ourselves**. This aspect of cleansing is mostly connected with intimacy with God and usefulness for service.

iii. "How can those expect God to purify their hearts who are continually indulging their *eyes*, *ears*, and *hands* in what is forbidden, and in what tends to increase and bring into action all the evil propensities of the soul?" (Clarke)

b. **From all filthiness of the flesh and spirit**: We often think of purity before the Lord only in terms of cleansing from **all filthiness of the flesh**, but there is also a **filthiness of the . . . spirit** to cleanse ourselves from.

i. Sometimes it is easier to deal with the **filthiness of the flesh** than the **filthiness . . . of the spirit**. During Jesus' earthly ministry, those who were stained by the **filthiness of the flesh** (such as harlots and tax collectors) found it easy to come to Jesus. But those stained by the **filthiness . . . of the spirit** (such as the scribes and Pharisees) found it very hard to come to Jesus.

ii. Our pride, our legalism, our self-focus, our self-righteousness, our bitterness, and our hatred can all be far worse to deal with than the more obvious sins of the flesh. "There is a defilement of the spirit which is independent of the defilement of the flesh. The spirit can be defiled in many ways. I sometimes think that the sins of the spirit are more deadly than the sins of the flesh." (Morgan)

iii. "I wish we were more concerned about cleansing ourselves from the filthiness of the spirit. I am inclined to think that some men heedlessly pollute their spirits; I mean that they do it willfully." (Spurgeon)

c. **Perfecting holiness in the fear of God**: This is something to *add*. Paul isn't writing about some state of sinless perfection. **Perfecting** has the idea of "complete" and "whole." Instead of a state of sinless perfection, Paul writes about a complete, "whole," holiness.

i. It isn't enough to only **cleanse ourselves from all filthiness**. The Christian life is not only getting rid of evil but continually doing and becoming good.

d. **Cleanse ourselves**: Note that Paul includes himself among the Corinthian Christians in the category of those who need to be cleansed. If Paul includes himself among those who needed to be cleansed, then what about us?

i. "I suppose that, the nearer we get to heaven, the more conscious we shall be of our imperfections. The more light we get, the more we discover our own darkness. That which is scarcely accounted sin by some men, will be a grievous defilement to a tender conscience. It is not that we are greater sinners as we grow older, but that we have a finer sensibility of sin, and see that to be sin which we winked at in the days of our ignorance." (Spurgeon)

ii. "I remember hearing a man say that he had lived for six years without having sinned in either thought, or word, or deed. I apprehended that he committed a sin then, if he had never done so before, in uttering such a proud, boastful speech." (Spurgeon)

iii. But we must take care that we **cleanse ourselves** and not concern ourselves with *cleansing others*. Most of the time we are more concerned with the holiness of others than our own holiness! "It were more in accordance with our tastes to cleanse other people, and attempt a moral reformation among our neighbors. Oh! it is easy to find out other men's faults, and to bring the whole force of our mind to inveigh against them." (Spurgeon)

B. Personal words about Paul's relationship with the Corinthians.

1. (2-3) Paul's appeal: **Open your hearts to us.**

Open *your hearts* to us. We have wronged no one, we have corrupted no one, we have cheated no one. I do not say *this* to condemn; for I have said before that you are in our hearts, to die together and to live together.

a. **Open your hearts**: In 2 Corinthians 6:11-13, Paul wrote: *We have spoken openly to you, our heart is wide open . . . you also be open.* Then, in 2 Corinthians 6:14-7:1, he dealt with the worldliness that kept the Corinthians from having the kind of open relationship they should have with Paul. Now, in writing **open your hearts to us**, Paul returns to idea he left off with in 2 Corinthians 6:11-13.

i. Paul was completely honest with the Corinthian Christians. Now he tells them they must be honest also and be **open** to seeing the truth about Paul and his ministry.

ii. The Corinthian Christians believed many bad things about Paul - that God wasn't using him, that he didn't have the kind of image, authority, or power an apostle should have - but their problem was not an information problem. Their problem was with their **hearts**. Their hearts had been open to the world but not to Paul. In the "unequally yoked" passage, Paul told them to close their hearts to the world. Now it is time to open their hearts to him.

b. **We have wronged no one, we have corrupted no one, we have defrauded no one**. Paul reminds the Corinthians of what they already know: Despite what some troublemakers said about Paul, they had no good reason to criticize him.

i. When Paul claims he **defrauded no one**, remember that he was organizing a collection for poor Christians in Judea and had responsibility over a significant amount of money (1 Corinthians 16:1-4).

c. **I do not say this to condemn**: Paul's desire isn't to condemn the Corinthian Christians but to restore the bonds of fellowship he once had with them. Paul really loved the Corinthian Christians: **I have said before that you are in our hearts, to die together and to live together**.

i. Paul *confronted* the Corinthian Christians, but he did not want to **condemn** them. It is possible to confront without condemning, though those who are being confronted rarely think so.

2. (4-7) Paul is encouraged by good news from the Corinthian Christians.

Great *is* my boldness of speech toward you, great *is* my boasting on your behalf. I am filled with comfort. I am exceedingly joyful in all our tribulation. For indeed, when we came to Macedonia, our bodies had no rest, but we were troubled on every side. Outside *were* conflicts, inside *were* fears. Nevertheless God, who comforts the downcast, comforted us by the coming of Titus, and not only by his coming, but also by the consolation with which he was comforted in you, when he told us of your earnest desire, your mourning, your zeal for me, so that I rejoiced even more.

a. **Great is my boldness of speech toward you, great is my boasting on your behalf**: Yes, Paul has been bold in his criticism to the Corinthians, but he was also bold in his **boasting** about them.

b. **I am filled with comfort. I am exceedingly joyful in all our tribulation . . . when he told us of your earnest desire, your zeal for me, so that I rejoiced even more**: Despite the many trials Paul faced (from both within and without), he found joy, and part of that joy was good news from the Corinthian Christians.

i. **I am exceedingly joyful in all our tribulation**: This phrase **exceedingly joyful** could be expressed as "I super-abound in joy; I have a joy beyond expression." Some think that God wants us to endure tribulation with a blank, stoic face - the "stiff upper lip" - but God wants more from us than that. He wants us to super-abound in joy even **in all our tribulation**.

ii. God brought comfort to Paul by hearing about the work God did among the Corinthian Christians. "No circumstances of personal affliction can dim the gladness of seeing souls grow in the grace of the Lord Jesus." (Morgan)

iii. When Paul speaks of **the coming of Titus**, he actually picks up where he left off in 2 Corinthians 2:13. In a sense, 2 Corinthians 2:14 to 7:4 is one long digression - led by God of course and containing some of the richest treasure of the New Testament.

c. **Our flesh had no rest, but we were troubled on every side**: Paul had a hard time in Macedonia, but Titus came to Paul when he was in Macedonia and he brought a good report of how the Corinthian Christians were turning back to Jesus and to Paul.

i. In spite of all his frustrations with the Corinthians and in the midst of all his afflictions in ministry, Paul had real confidence and hope because Titus brought him a good report of how things were going in Corinth.

ii. In 2 Corinthians 1:3, Paul declared that God is the **God of all comfort**. Here, Paul experienced that comfort through the coming of Titus and the news from Corinth. Paul experienced the comfort of God through human instruments. Often when we turn away from people, we turn away from the comfort God wants to give us.

d. **Outside were conflicts, inside were fears**: This was Paul's life in ministry. It was a life of great blessing but also a life of many **conflicts** and **fears**. On the **outside**, Paul was constantly in conflict with enemies of the gospel and worldly minded Christians. On the **inside**, Paul daily battled with the stress and anxiety of ministry.

e. **Your earnest desire, your mourning, your zeal for me**: Titus told Paul that the Corinthian Christians had not forsaken him completely. In fact, these things (**desire . . . mourning . . . zeal**) proved God really was doing a work in the Corinthian Christians, and knowing that was a comfort to Paul.

3. (8-12) The severe letter and its effect.

For even if I made you sorry with my letter, I do not regret it; though I did regret it. For I perceive that the same epistle made you sorry, though only for a while. Now I rejoice, not that you were made sorry, but that your sorrow led to repentance. For you were made sorry in a godly manner, that you might suffer loss from us in nothing. For godly sorrow produces repentance *leading* to salvation, not to be regretted; but the sorrow of the world produces death. For observe this very thing,

that you sorrowed in a godly manner: What diligence it produced in you, *what* clearing *of yourselves*, *what* indignation, *what* fear, *what* vehement desire, *what* zeal, *what* vindication! In all *things* you proved yourselves to be clear in this matter. Therefore, although I wrote to you, *I did* not *do it* for the sake of him who had done the wrong, nor for the sake of him who suffered wrong, but that our care for you in the sight of God might appear to you.

a. **For even if I made you sorry with my letter**: What **letter?** This probably is not the letter of 1 Corinthians but a letter that Paul wrote in between 1 and 2 Corinthians.

i. It helps if we remember the sequence of events. Things were going badly among the Christians in Corinth, and in an attempt to get them on track, Paul made a quick, unplanned visit that only seemed to make things worse (the "sorrowful visit" mentioned in 2 Corinthians 2:1). After the failure of this visit, Paul decided not to visit Corinth again in person at the time but instead sent Titus to them with a strong letter of rebuke. Paul was very worried about how the Corinthians would receive the letter and whether it would turn them to Jesus or just make them angry. When Titus came back with good news from the Corinthian Christians, Paul was greatly relieved.

b. **I do not regret it; though I did regret it**: When Paul first wrote the "sorrowful letter" carried by Titus, he didn't enjoy the idea of being so confrontational with the Corinthian Christians, even though they deserved it. That's why he wrote, "**though I did regret it.**" At the same time, when Titus came back and reported the response of the Corinthian Christians (the *earnest desire . . . mourning* and *zeal* mentioned in 2 Corinthians 7:7), Paul was happy for the effect the letter had. That's why he wrote, "**I do not regret it.**"

c. **The same epistle made you sorry, though only for a while**: "In sin, the pleasure passeth, the sorrow remaineth; but in repentance, the sorrow passeth, the pleasure abideth for ever. God soon poureth the oil of gladness into broken hearts." (Trapp)

d. **Not that you were made sorry, but that your sorrow led to repentance.** Paul makes a clear separation between **sorrow** and **repentance**. They are not the same things! One can be *sorry* for their sin without *repenting* from their sin. **Sorrow** describes a feeling, but **repentance** describes change in both the mind and in the life.

i. "Repentance is not sorrow only. It may be unaccompanied by sorrow . . . at the time, but sorrow will always follow, sorrow for the past; but this change of mind is the great thing." (Morgan)

ii. "Sorrow alone accomplishes nothing. Peter was sorry he denied Christ, and he repented. Judas was sorry he betrayed Christ but, instead of repenting, he killed himself." (Smith)

iii. **"Repentance"** sounds like a harsh word to many but it is an essential aspect of the gospel and has been called "the first word of the gospel." When John the Baptist preached, he said *Repent, for the kingdom of heaven is at hand!* (Matthew 3:2). When Jesus began to preach, He said *Repent, for the kingdom of heaven is at hand* (Matthew 4:17). When Peter preached on the day of Pentecost, he told his listeners to *repent* (Acts 2:38).

iv. What was it that the Corinthian Christians had to repent of? Take your pick! It could have been any number of things, but no doubt it also included this: There were probably some "anti-Paul" people who criticized the absent apostle severely and unfairly, and the Corinthians did not defend their godly spiritual father before these detractors.

e. **You were made sorry in a godly manner**: Paul made the Corinthian Christians feel bad for their sin, but he did it in a godly way. He used the truth, not lies or exaggeration. He was honest, not using hidden agendas and manipulation. He simply told the truth in love. Not every preacher or every person can say they do the same as Paul did and it isn't right to try to make someone **sorry** in an un**godly manner**.

i. **That you might suffer loss from us in nothing** shows *why* it is important to *only* make others **sorrow in a godly manner**. You may succeed in making them feel bad (**sorrow**), but the relationship you have with that person will **suffer loss**. You can win the "battle" yet lose the "war." Paul wanted to protect his relationship with the Corinthian Christians, so he would only make them **sorry in a godly manner**.

f. **Godly sorrow produces repentance unto salvation**: Does this mean we are saved by our repentance? Not exactly. Repentance "is not the ground of our salvation; but it is a part of it and necessary condition of it. Those who repent are saved; the impenitent perish. Repentance is therefore *unto salvation*." (Hodge)

i. Repentance must never be thought of as something we must do *before* we can come back to God. Repentance describes the very act of coming to God. You can't turn *towards* God without turning *from* the things He is against. "People seem to jump into faith very quickly nowadays. I do not disapprove of that happy leap; but still, I hope my old friend repentance is not dead. I am desperately in love with repentance; it seems to me to be the twin-sister to faith." (Spurgeon)

ii. Sorrow in itself doesn't produce anything except bad feelings, but **godly sorrow produces repentance**. Since repentance is a change (in both thinking and action), we can tell if sorrow is really **godly** by seeing if it **produces repentance**. So **godly sorrow** cannot be measured by feelings or tears, only by what it **produces**.

iii. "How sorry do you think you have to be? What is the purpose of your sorrow for sin? It is to bring you to trust in the atoning work of our Lord Jesus Christ. It is not your sorrow that cleanses you from sin, but His blood. It is the goodness of God that leads a man to repentance. Has your sorrow for sin led you at one time or another fling all the burden of it at the feet of a crucified, risen Saviour? If it hasn't, anything short of that is what Paul here calls sorrow that leads to death." (Redpath)

iv. Real repentance acts. "If thou repent with a contradiction (saith Tertullian) God will pardon thee with a contradiction. Thou repentest, and yet continuest in thy sin. God will pardon thee, and yet send thee to hell. There is pardon with a contradiction." (John Trapp wrote these hard and striking words)

g. **Not to be regretted**: This is because **godly sorrow** does such a great work. It doesn't feel good, but it does a good work. The **sorrow of the world** is different, because it **produces death**.

i. When sorrow is received or borne in a worldly way, it has the deadly effect of producing resentment or bitterness. We can regret that kind of sorrow. Godly sorrow produces repentance unto salvation that is **not to be regretted**. "A repentance as a man shall never have cause to repent of. Job cursed the day of his birth; but no man was ever heard to curse the day of his new birth." (Trapp)

ii. "In repentance there is a bitter sweetness, or a sweet bitterness - which shall I call it? - of which, the more you have, the better it is for you. I can truly say that I hardly know a diviner joy than to lay my head in my Heavenly Father's bosom and to say, 'Father, I have sinned, but thou hast forgiven me; and, oh, I do love thee!' " (Spurgeon)

h. **What diligence it produced in you, what clearing of yourselves, what indignation, what fear, what vehement desire, what zeal, what vindication!** All of these things showed that the sorrow of the Corinthian Christians worked real repentance.

i. **What diligence**: Godly sorrow produces, and repentance shows **diligence**. Repentance means to turn around, and it takes **diligence** to stay turned around. If one gives up easily, they can never *walk* in repentance, though they may perform *acts* of repentance.

ii. **What clearing of yourselves**: Godly sorrow produces, and repentance shows a **clearing**. It is a clearing of guilt and shame, from knowing that we brought our sin to God and we now walk in the right way.

iii. **What indignation**: Godly sorrow produces, and repentance shows **indignation**. We are indignant at our selves for our foolishness in sin. This is the kind of attitude that makes repentance last. "I am glad that the Bible allows me to get mad, mad with the devil! To think that he had the audacity to pull me down and make me do that! What indignation, what fury at sin and all the agencies of Satan!" (Redpath)

iv. **What fear**: Godly sorrow produces, and repentance shows a **fear** that we would ever fall into the same sin again. Paul isn't writing about a *fear of God* here as much as a *fear of sin*, and fear of our own weakness toward sin.

v. **What vehement desire**: Godly sorrow produces, and repentance shows **vehement desire**. This is a heart that really desires purity and godliness and does not want to sin any more. This **vehement desire** is expressed through heartfelt prayer and total dependence on God.

vi. **What zeal**: Godly sorrow produces, and repentance shows **zeal**. The ancient Greek word speaks of *heat*; we are hot *towards* God and His righteousness, and hot *against* sin and impurity. Instead of laziness, we have **zeal** in our walk with the Lord.

vii. **What vindication**: Godly sorrow produces, and repentance shows **vindication**. You are vindicated as a Christian, even though you have sinned. No one can doubt it because the measure of a Christian is not whether or not they sin, but whether or not they *repent*.

viii. **Proved yourself to be clear**: When repentance is marked by the preceding characteristics, we are **clear** of guilt and sin. The stain of sin is gone! We can feel it, and others can see it. "Happy is that man who has had enough of the smart of sin to make it sour and bitter to him all the rest of his days; so that now, with changed heart, and renewed spirit, he perseveres in the ways of God, never thinking of going back, but resolved 'through floods or flames' to force his way to heaven, to be, by divine grace, master over every sin that assails him." (Spurgeon)

i. **In all things you proved yourselves to be clear**: Their actions of repentance **proved** them **to be clear**. It wasn't words or feelings that **proved** them **to be clear**, but actions.

i. "Godly sorrow that leads to repentance, therefore, is a sorrow that leads to a change of purpose, of intention, and of action. It is not the sorrow of idle tears; it is not crying by your bedside because once again you have failed; nor is it vain regret, wishing things had never happened, wishing you could live the moments again. No, it is not that. It is a change of purpose and intentions, a change of direction and action." (Redpath)

j. **In this matter**: Paul is using godly discretion by not bringing up the whole affair again from the beginning. There was someone who had done wrong (**him who had done the wrong**) and there was someone who had been wronged (**him who suffered wrong**). But there was no need to go through the whole mess again.

k. **I did not do it for the sake**: Paul's purpose in writing the "sorrowful letter" was not to take sides in a dispute among the Corinthian Christians. His purpose was to demonstrate his concern (**that our care for you in the sight of God might appear to you**).

i. Paul's concern for the Corinthian Christians was evident but amazing. "From all appearance there was never a Church less worthy of an apostle's affections than this Church was at this time; and yet no one ever more beloved." (Clarke)

4. (13-16) How Titus regarded the Corinthian Christians after his visit.

Therefore we have been comforted in your comfort. And we rejoiced exceedingly more for the joy of Titus, because his spirit has been refreshed by you all. For if in anything I have boasted to him about you, I am not ashamed. But as we spoke all things to you in truth, even so our boasting to Titus was found true. And his affections are greater for you as he remembers the obedience of you all, how with fear and trembling you received him. Therefore I rejoice that I have confidence in you in everything.

a. **His spirit has been refreshed by you all**: The experience of Titus in Corinth and his report from there were sure evidence that the Corinthian Christians had a change of mind.

b. **If in anything I have boasted to him about you**: Paul had "hopefully" boasted to Titus that the Corinthian Christians would respond well to the severe letter. Probably Titus was not so sure! But Paul's **boasting to Titus was found true**.

c. **His affections are great for you**: Paul assures the Corinthian Christians that Titus loves them more than ever now. Probably Titus saw a lot of ugliness among the Corinthian Christians, and from this he may have had a "chip on his shoulder" against them. So Paul wants them to know that after he saw and reported their repentance, Titus loved them more than ever.

d. **I rejoice that I have confidence in you in everything**: Is Paul being sarcastic here? Probably not. He is probably simply trying to encourage the Corinthians, showing them that he is convinced their repentance was genuine.

> i. "Thus by praising them, he further winneth upon them, whom before he had more sharply handled. Sour and sweet make the best sauce." (Trapp)

> ii. At the end of this chapter, Paul praises the Corinthian Christians and they seem to be in a place of victory. But in the "sorrowful letter" (mentioned in 2 Corinthians 2:1) there was no praise. What was the difference? Their real repentance, reported by Titus and commented on by Paul in this chapter.

> iii. All through this chapter we see how concerned Paul was about his relationship with the Corinthian Christians. This shows that *people* were just as important to Paul as *ministry*. He didn't want to do "ministry" at the expense of his relationships with people.

2 Corinthians 8 - Encouragement and Examples in Giving

A. Examples and encouragement.

1. (1-5) The example of the Macedonian Christians.

Moreover, brethren, we make known to you the grace of God bestowed on the churches of Macedonia: that in a great trial of affliction the abundance of their joy and their deep poverty abounded in the riches of their liberality. For I bear witness that according to *their* ability, yes, and beyond *their* ability, *they were* freely willing, imploring us with much urgency that we would receive the gift and the fellowship of the ministering to the saints. And not *only* as we had hoped, but they first gave themselves to the Lord, and *then* to us by the will of God.

a. **The grace of God**: Paul will now write about other churches and their example in giving. In his first few words on this subject, Paul shows he considers both the *opportunity* and the *willingness* to give a gift from **the grace of God**.

b. **The churches of Macedonia**: The northern part of Greece was called **Macedonia**. The southern part was called *Achaia*, and the city of Corinth was in the region of Achaia. Paul writes about the example he sees in **the churches of Macedonia**. The **churches of Macedonia** were in cities such as Philippi, Thessalonica, and Berea.

c. **That in a great trial of affliction the abundance of their joy and their deep poverty abounded in the riches of their liberality**: Paul reports to the Corinthian Christians the example of the Macedonian Christians. The Macedonians, though they were in **a great trial of affliction** and though they were in **deep poverty**, still gave generously (**abounded in the riches of their liberality**).

i. Why did Paul write about giving at all? What was he collecting money for? Paul was raising money to help the Christians in Jerusalem, who were very poor. He had previously mentioned this effort in 1 Corinthians 16:1-4.

ii. The poverty of the Macedonians is confirmed by secular history. The Romans took most of their wealth when they conquered this former homeland of Alexander the Great.

d. **For I bear witness**: Paul knew that the Macedonians gave in two ways. First, they gave **according to their ability** in the sense that in total, their gift wasn't very much. It was not a "large" gift in a total dollar sense. Secondly, since their heart was **freely willing to give**, and they gave in proportion to the little they did have, they gave **beyond their ability**.

i. The account of the widow's giving in Luke 21:1-4 illustrates the same point. She only gave *two mites*, which was a very small amount of money. In that sense, she gave **according to** [her] **ability**. Nevertheless, since she gave all she had - after all, she might have kept one mite to herself - she gave **beyond** [her] **ability**. The same principle of giving was evident in the Macedonian Christians.

ii. "That poor widow's mite was beyond the rich man's magnificence, because it came out of a richer mind." (Trapp)

e. **Freely willing, imploring us with much urgency that we would receive the gift**: Paul didn't have to beg for money from the Macedonian Christians (which he wouldn't have done anyway). Instead, they were *begging him* (**imploring us**) to **receive the gift**!

i. **Imploring us** means that it was the Macedonians who begged Paul for the privilege of giving, not Paul who begged them for money.

ii. So, though the Macedonian Christians didn't have much to give, they really *wanted* to give. They saw it as a *privilege* to give. True Christian generosity can't be measured by how much one has to give. Often those who have less are more generous with what they have.

iii. "The example of the Macedonians is practical proof that true generosity is not the prerogative of those who enjoy an adequacy of means. The most genuine liberality is frequently displayed by those who have least to give. Christian giving is estimated in terms not of quantity but of sacrifice." (Hughes)

f. **Not as we hoped**: The Macedonian Christians gave far beyond what Paul hoped for. What made their giving so spectacular? It wasn't the dollar amount. It was that they **first gave themselves to the Lord, and then to us by the will of God**. Why were the Macedonians such good examples of giving? Because they **first gave themselves to the Lord**; then they gave their trust to Paul and the other apostles.

> i. In giving, the real issue isn't giving money. It is giving ourselves to the Lord. If we really give ourselves to the Lord, then the right kind of material giving will naturally follow.

2. (6-8) Paul's tender, wise encouragement in giving.

So we urged Titus, that as he had begun, so he would also complete this grace in you as well. But as you abound in everything; in faith, in speech, in knowledge, in all diligence, and in your love for us; *see* that you abound in this grace also. I speak not by commandment, but I am testing the sincerity of your love by the diligence of others.

a. **So we urged Titus, that as he had begun, so he would also complete this grace in you as well**: Paul's associate, Titus, as the bearer of this letter, was supposed to encourage the Corinthian Christians to actually give him the collection, then he would give it to Paul. He was supposed to make certain that they actually followed through on what they had intended to do earlier.

> i. We might imagine that the Corinthian Christians were willing to take up a collection for the saints in Jerusalem and give that money to Paul to take with him to Jerusalem. But when things became difficult between Paul and the Corinthian Christians, they may have been less willing to take up the collection and put it in Paul's hands. One reason Titus was sent with this letter was to **complete this grace** in the Corinthian Christians and make certain they followed through on their original intent.

> ii. **Complete this grace**: The Corinthian Christians may have *intended* to give. They may have *thought* about giving. They may have been *favorable to the idea* of giving. Yet all of this was useless unless they did in fact **complete this grace**. Our intentions, vows, and resolutions are useless without action. It was time for the Corinthian Christians to act, and Titus was sent to help them do this.

b. **As you abound in everything**: Is Paul being sarcastic here? Probably. If the Corinthian Christians did indeed abound **in faith, in speech, in knowledge, in all diligence, and in . . . love for** Paul, they had just started to do these things. But the Corinthian Christians probably *thought of themselves* as abounding in all those things. So it is as if Paul is saying, "Very well, I'll take your word for it. You do abound in all these things. So now, **abound in this grace also**."

i. **This grace also**: Now, for the fourth time since the beginning of the chapter, Paul refers to giving money as a **grace** (*grace of God . . . receive the gift . . . complete this grace*). The fact that Paul uses the ancient Greek word *charis* to describe financial giving means a few things.

ii. *The ability to give and the heart to give is a free gift from God.* Giving is a work of God's grace in us. When you see a believer who is truly generous, a great work of God has been done in their heart. We should never say, "Well, they just want to write the checks and not get involved." No, giving *is* getting involved, and it demonstrates a true work of God's grace in the heart.

iii. *Our giving should be like God's giving of grace to us: giving freely, generously, because we want to give.* When God gives to us out of grace, the motive for His giving is in *Him*, not based in the one who receives. That is how we should give - because the motive of the love and generosity of God is so big in our heart that we simply *must* give.

iv. *Our giving, like God's grace to us, should be offered without expectation of payment in return.* God does not give to us expecting "payback." We can never repay God. We can just serve Him and love Him in return.

v. "Once you see the matter of giving is centered in this lovely word *grace*, it lifts the whole act away from mechanics, from pressure and duty, from obligation and mere legalism. It lifts us up into the most lovely atmosphere of an activity which seeks by giving to convey to others all that is lovely, all that is beautiful, all that is good, and all that is glorious. What a lovely word this word is . . . For there is no area in the Christian life in which grace shines out so much, so beautifully, so delightfully, and so happily as when giving comes from the background of poverty." (Redpath)

c. **I speak not by commandment**: Paul isn't commanding the Corinthian Christians to give. Paul knew that giving from commandment isn't giving at all; we call that kind of giving *taxation*.

d. **I am testing the sincerity of your love by the diligence of others**: Paul makes two important points here. First, giving can measure the **sincerity of your love**. Second, Paul openly *compared* the giving of the Corinthian Christians to the giving of the Macedonian Christians (**testing the sincerity of your love by the diligence of others**).

i. Many of us like to think that we can love without giving, but what does 1 John 3:17-18 say? *Whoever has this world's goods, and sees his brother in need, and shuts up his heart from him, how does the love of God abide in him? My little children, let us not love in word or in tongue, but in deed and in truth.* Jesus said much the same in Matthew 6:21: *For where your treasure is, there your heart will be also.* What we give, and how we follow through on our commitment to give, are valid tests of our love.

ii. Also, it is not unfair to compare our giving with the giving of others, at least in some sense. Jesus compared the giving of the poor widow with the giving of others (Luke 21:1-4). But we shouldn't think that Paul is encouraging a fund-raising competition between the churches of Macedonia and Corinth. He simply uses the Macedonians (who gave so much even in their poverty) as an example of giving.

iii. Since the Corinthians had more than the Macedonians did, they *should* give more. Calvin puts it plainly: "Rich men owe God a large tribute and poor men have no reason to be ashamed if what they give is small."

3. (9) The second example of giving: **our Lord Jesus**.

For you know the grace of our Lord Jesus Christ, that though He was rich, yet for your sakes He became poor, that you through His poverty might become rich.

a. **You know the grace of our Lord Jesus**: From the context, and from how Paul has used the word **grace** in this passage, we know that Paul means, "You know the *giving* of our Lord Jesus."

b. **Though He was rich**: When was Jesus **rich**? Before He added humanity to His deity and walked this earth. Here, Paul subtly, but definitely, points to the deity of Jesus. There is no way Paul could write **though He was rich** if Jesus began His existence in Mary's womb.

i. And what riches! Jesus, as the eternal Second Member of the Trinity, as God the Son, living in the riches and splendor of the ivory palaces of heaven (Psalm 45:8), surrounded constantly by the glory, power, and majesty of God. The riches Jesus enjoyed before adding humanity to His deity make *any* amount of wealth on earth seem poor.

ii. Notice that it says that Jesus **became poor** when **He was rich**. Just as Jesus added humanity but never lost His deity, so He also "added" poverty but never "lost" His riches. "For He assumed poverty, yet did not lose His riches. Inwardly He was rich, outwardly poor. His deity was hidden in His riches, His manhood apparent in His poverty." (Hughes)

c. **Yet for your sakes He became poor**: Jesus lived His earthly life as a poor man. We should not exaggerate the poverty of Jesus; after all, He was not a destitute beggar. Yet He could say of Himself, *"Foxes have holes and birds of the air have nests, but the Son of Man has nowhere to lay His head."* (Matthew 8:20)

i. When we contrast the simple life of Jesus (**He became poor**) with His existence before adding humanity to His deity (**He was rich**), we are even more amazed. Poverty always feels worse when one has been rich.

ii. Most amazing of all is *why* Jesus accepted this simple life of poverty: **for your sakes**. This was Jesus' "giving." He gave financially in the sense that He accepted a humble life of poverty (when He had all power to live as the wealthiest man in all history), and He did it **for [our] sakes**.

iii. Why would Jesus need to become poor **for your sakes**? How does His poverty benefit us?

- Because it shows us the giving heart of God

- Because it shows us the relative importance of material things

- Because it makes Jesus open and accessible to all

- Because it rebukes the pride that might refuse to come to a poor Savior

- Because it gave others the privilege of giving to Jesus

- Because it fulfilled the heart and will and plan of God, making our salvation possible

d. **That you through His poverty might become rich**: Because of Jesus' poverty and all that was related to it, we can **become rich**. We have a share in Jesus' eternal, heavenly wealth because He came and had a share in our poverty.

B. Practical words of advice regarding giving.

1. (10-12) Follow through on your previous willingness.

And in this I give advice: It is to your advantage not only to be doing what you began and were desiring to do a year ago; but now you also must complete the doing *of it*; that as *there was* a readiness to desire *it*, so *there* also *may be* a completion out of what *you* have. For if there is first a willing mind, *it is* accepted according to what one has, *and* not according to what he does not have.

a. **Now you also must complete the doing of it**: The Corinthian Christians previously expressed a **desiring** and a **readiness** to give. Now, they *actually had to do it!*

i. The Devil will let you *resolve* as much as you like - the more the better - just as long as you never carry it out. "The tragedy of life so often is, not that we have no high impulses, but that we fail to turn them into actions." (Barclay)

ii. John Trapp wrote more than 300 years ago, "This age aboundeth with mouth-mercy, which is good cheap, and therefore like refuse fruit is found growing in every hedge. But a little handful were worth a great many such mouthfuls." How much truer is this today!

b. **A completion out of what you have**: We can't give what we don't have. God judges our giving against what resources we have. However, the issue of *what and how we spend* is relevant to **what you have**. If you over-spend and therefore never have any to give, you can't excuse it before God by saying, "Well, I don't have anything to give."

c. **If there is first a willing mind**: When we give, God looks for **readiness** and **a willing mind**. These are the true marks of a generous heart before God and are no more likely among the rich than the poor.

d. **It is accepted according to what one has, and not according to what he does not have**: Again, God does not expect us to give what we do not have. True Christian giving cannot be measured by the amount. One might give a million dollars and yet not give enough; another may give one dollar and give with tremendous sacrifice and generosity. True giving is measured by obedience, proportion, and need, not by amount.

i. When the issue of giving is brought up many ask, "How much am I supposed to give?" Paul's principles throughout this letter and other letters remind us that there is no one answer to that question for every believer.

ii. Many go back to the Old Testament law of the tithe, the giving of ten percent unto the Lord. This is a good principle for giving and perhaps a broad benchmark, yet the New Testament nowhere specifically commands tithing. The New Testament certainly does speak of tithing in a positive light if it is done with a right heart (Luke 11:42).

iii. But the New Testament speaks with great clarity on the principles of *giving*. It teaches us that giving should be *regular, planned, proportional,* and *private* (1 Corinthians 16:1-4) and that it must be *generous, freely given*, and *cheerful* (2 Corinthians 9).

iv. Since the New Testament doesn't emphasize tithing, one might not be strict on it for Christians (though some Christians do argue against tithing on the basis of self-interest). However, since giving should be *proportional*, we should give *some* percentage, and ten percent is a good benchmark or goal. However, for some to give ten percent is nowhere near enough; for others, at their present time, five percent may be a massive step of faith.

v. If our question is, "How little can I give and still be pleasing to God?" our heart isn't in the right place at all. We should have the attitude of some early Christians, who essentially said: "We're not under the tithe - we can give *more!*" Giving and financial management are *spiritual* issues, not only financial issues (Luke 16:11).

2. (13-15) Understand the cause you give to.

For *I do* not *mean* that others should be eased and you burdened; but by an equality, *that* now at this time your abundance *may supply* their lack, that their abundance also may supply your lack; that there may be equality. As it is written, "He who *gathered* much had nothing left over, and he who *gathered* little had no lack."

a. **For I do not mean that others should be eased and you burdened**: The Corinthian Christians were not giving so that the Jerusalem Christians would get rich and lazy at their expense. Paul was taking the collection so the Jerusalem Christians could merely survive. The goal was not to *burden* the Corinthian Christians, nor was it to make it *easy* for the Jerusalem Christians.

i. Some like to say, "Give till it hurts. Then keep giving until it feels better again." But God's goal for us isn't to "Give till it hurts." The goal is not to afflict those who give, it is to display the giving heart and love of Jesus Christ.

ii. "This teaching is needed to refute fanatics who think that you have done nothing unless you strip yourself completely and put everything into a common fund." (Calvin)

b. **But by an equality**: Paul sees that the *spiritual* **abundance** of the Jerusalem Christians has blessed the Corinthian Christians. Therefore, it should be a small thing for the Corinthian Christians to share with them their *material* **abundance**.

i. The **equality** Paul mentions here isn't meant to imply socialism or communism, where all are said to live at the same economic level, and none are supposed to be richer than others are. Of course, communism and socialism themselves are evil, being noble ideas in theory but absolute tyrannies when sharing is commanded at the end of a gun. But this is not the kind of equality Paul means anyway. "I acknowledge indeed that we are not bound to such an equality as would make it wrong for the rich to live more elegantly than the poor; but there must be an equality that nobody starves and nobody hordes his abundance at another's expense." (Calvin)

ii. "Thus do the Scriptures avoid, on the one hand, the injustice and destructive evils of agrarian communism, by recognizing the right of property and making all almsgiving optional; and on the other, the heartless disregard of the poor by inculcating the universal brother-hood of believers, and the consequent duty of each to contribute of his abundance to relieve the necessities of the poor. At the same time they inculcate on the poor the duty of self-support to the extent of their ability." (Hodge)

c. **Now at this time** reminds the Corinthian Christians that this is just the way it is right now. There may be a time later when the spiritual abundance of the Corinthian Christians may minister to the saints in Jerusalem, and the material abundance of the saints in Jerusalem ministers to the Corinthian Christians.

i. But there is no idea of Jerusalem giving "spiritual" riches in ex-change for material help. The saints in Jerusalem were not "selling" spiritual things. "Such an idea as that of the transference of the mer-its of the saints is, of course, quite foreign to the context." (Bernard)

d. **He who gathered much had nothing left over, and he who gath-ered little had no lack:** Paul's quotation from Exodus 16:18 illustrates his principle. Everyone gathered what they could, some more and some less; but they all shared what they gathered.

i. Hodge makes the point well: "Property is like manna, it will not bear hoarding."

ii. "All that we have is manna . . . And just as manna, which was hoarded to excess out of greed or lack of faith, immediately putrefied, so we should have no doubt that riches which are heaped up at the expense of our brethren are accursed and will soon perish and their owner will be ruined with them." (Calvin)

3. (16-24) How to receive Titus when he and his companions come for the collection.

But thanks *be* to God who puts the same earnest care for you into the heart of Titus. For he not only accepted the exhortation, but being more diligent, he went to you of his own accord. And we have sent with him the brother whose praise *is* in the gospel throughout all the churches, and not only *that*, but who was also chosen by the churches to travel with us with this gift, which is administered by us to the glory of the Lord Himself and *to show* your ready mind, avoiding this: that anyone should blame us in this lavish gift which is administered by us; provid-ing honorable things, not only in the sight of the Lord, but also in the sight of men. And we have sent with them our brother whom we have often proved diligent in many things, but now much more diligent, be-cause of the great confidence which *we have* in you. If *anyone inquires* about Titus, *he is* my partner and fellow worker concerning you. Or if

our brethren *are inquired about, they are* **messengers of the churches, the glory of Christ. Therefore show to them, and before the churches the proof of your love and of our boasting on your behalf.**

a. **But thanks be to God who pus the same earnest care for you into the heart of Titus**: Paul's intention is to recommend Titus to them as a trustworthy bearer of their money.

b. **And we have sent with him the brother whose praise is in the gospel throughout all the churches**: Commentators have had a field day trying to identify the **brother** mentioned here. Who is he?

i. This **brother** accompanied Titus when he went to Corinth on Paul's behalf.

ii. This **brother** was well known and praised **in the gospel** in **all the churches**.

iii. This **brother** was **also chosen by the churches to travel with** Paul, carrying **the gift**. Beyond these things we know nothing about this man.

iv. As you might expect, Bible commentators have been ready to say whom they believe **the brother** to be. Some of the candidates have been Luke, Barnabas, Silas, Timothy, and a variety of others, but no one really knows. We can confidently say that it doesn't really matter, otherwise, God would have made it clear.

c. **Avoiding this: that anyone should blame us in this lavish gift**: Paul wisely avoided any gossip about his role in the collection by sending Titus and his companion to collect it, and to accompany Paul in carrying it to Jerusalem.

i. **Also in the sight of men** is a reminder that all things financial in the church should be conducted above board and properly. Paul took whatever steps were necessary so no one could blame him with financial impropriety. Paul could write like a poet and think like a theologian; but he could also act with the meticulous accuracy and integrity of the best accountant.

d. **Therefore show to them, and before the churches, the proof of your love and of our boasting on your behalf**: This is a strong encouragement from Paul to give. He says that when Titus and the unnamed brother come, the Corinthians should **show** them a good offering.

• **Show** a good offering because **the churches** will also know about it and thank God for His work among the Corinthians

• **Show** a good offering because the offering given will be **proof of your love**

- **Show** a good offering because Paul has been **boasting** to others about what givers the Corinthian Christians had been

i. The concluding idea is clear. Paul asks them to now come through and give like the good givers he has claimed they are.

2 Corinthians 9 - How God Wants Us To Give

A. Be ready to give.

1. (1-2) The willingness of the Corinthian Christians to give.

Now concerning the ministering to the saints, it is superfluous for me to write to you; for I know your willingness, about which I boast of you to the Macedonians, that Achaia was ready a year ago; and your zeal has stirred up the majority.

a. **Concerning the ministering to the saints**: The specific **ministering** Paul has in mind is the financial support of the Jerusalem **saints**. Paul will be in Corinth to pick up this collection for the Jerusalem saints, which he wrote of in 2 Corinthians 8 and in other previous passages (such as 1 Corinthians 16:1-4).

i. In Acts 11:29, a previous collection for the Jerusalem saints is described: *Then the disciples, each according to his ability, determined to send relief to the brethren dwelling in Judea.* The ancient Greek word translated **ministering** (*diakonia*) is the same word translated *relief* in Acts 11:29.

ii. The same ancient Greek work for **ministering** is used in a spiritual sense in passages like 2 Corinthians 3:8-9 and is used in a practical sense in passages like 2 Corinthians 9:1.

b. **It is superfluous for me to write to you; for I know your willingness**: Here, Paul may be showing his sarcasm again. The basic idea is, "I don't even need to write this, reminding you about the collection, because you are already ready and willing to give." Of course, if the Corinthian Christians were really as ready and willing as Paul seems to indicate, he really wouldn't need to write this at all.

i. At the same time, this is a signal that Paul is done trying to persuade the Corinthian regarding giving, as he did in 2 Corinthians 8, showing the example of the Macedonian Christians and the example of Jesus. Now Paul is encouraging them in their *manner* of giving.

c. **About which I boast of you to the Macedonians**: In the previous chapter, Paul spoke of the **Macedonians** as wonderful examples of giving (2 Corinthians 8:1-8). Now, Paul (sarcastically?) informs the Corinthian Christians that he has boasted to the **Macedonians** about the Corinthian **willingness** to give.

i. This may be a "playful" way of encouraging the Corinthian Christians to really be ready and willing to give. Paul may be saying, "Come now, you really can be ready to give. After all, I've already bragged about your willingness to others!"

ii. **Macedonians . . . Achaia**: *Macedonia* and **Achaia** were regions on the Greek peninsula. *Macedonia* was to the north, and **Achaia** was to the south. Corinth was the leading city of the region of **Achaia**. The region of Macedonia had churches in cities such as Philippi, Berea, and Thessalonica.

d. **Your zeal has stirred up the majority**: Again, Paul seems to be sarcastic - or at least playful - here. He is saying that the Corinthian Christians were so zealous in their willingness to give that they were an example to **the majority** of other Christians. He says that essentially, the good example of the Macedonians (as related in 2 Corinthians 8:1-8) is just a reflection of the good example the Corinthian Christians presented to the Macedonians first.

i. We think Paul is being sarcastic here because if the Corinthians really were such great examples in giving, and if their giving prompted others to give, then Paul would never have to give them as much instruction and encouragement as he does in 2 Corinthians.

2. (3-5) Paul is sending Titus and the others to pick up the collection.

Yet I have sent the brethren, lest our boasting of you should be in vain in this respect, that, as I said, you may be ready; lest if *some* Macedonians come with me and find you unprepared, we (not to mention you!) should be ashamed of this confident boasting. Therefore I thought it necessary to exhort the brethren to go to you ahead of time, and prepare your generous gift beforehand, which *you had* previously promised, that it may be ready as *a matter* of generosity and not as a grudging obligation.

a. **Yet I have sent the brethren**: Paul again is giving a little sarcastic twist. It is as if he says, "You all are so ready and willing to give that I'm sure you would bring the collection to me. But in any regard, I'll send **the brethren** to come pick it up. After all, I don't want all my boasting about you to have been **in vain**."

2 Corinthians 9   109

b. **Lest if some Macedonians come with me and find you unprepared**: The playful sarcasm continues. "After all, Corinthians, you don't want the Macedonians to see that you were unwilling to give. We don't want a case where **we (not to mention you!) should be ashamed of this confident boasting**."

c. **Therefore I thought it necessary . . . that it may be ready as a matter of generosity and not as a grudging obligation**: Paul wanted the whole business of the collection completed before he arrived so that there would be nothing even remotely manipulative in his receiving the collection.

> i. Paul was very concerned that giving be a matter of **generosity** and not a matter of **grudging obligation**. God Himself never gives out of an attitude of **grudging obligation**, and neither should we. To be *generous*, in the Biblical idea of the word, has more to do with our *attitude* in giving than with the *amount* that we give, so God wants a willing attitude from givers.

> ii. "When God gives grace, He does not reluctantly open a little finger and maintain a clenched fist full of gifts. I would tell you today that God's hands are nail-pierced hands and they are wide open. This fountain of grace is always pouring itself out with no limitation on heaven's side at all." (Redpath)

B. The reward of giving and the right heart in giving.

1. (6) Our giving should be bountiful, if we would be rewarded bountifully.

But this *I* say: He who sows sparingly will also reap sparingly, and he who sows bountifully will also reap bountifully.

a. **He who sows sparingly will also reap sparingly**: A farmer sowing seed may feel he loses seed as it falls from his hand to the ground, and we may feel we are losing when we give. But just as the farmer gives the seed it in anticipation of a future harvest, we should give with the same heart.

> i. If a farmer planted only a few seeds because he wanted to "hold on" to as much seed as he could, he would have more seed in his barn after sowing time. But at the harvest, the one who planted more seed would have much more grain in his barn.

b. **Will also reap bountifully**: What do we reap when we give? We reap blessings that are both *material* and *spiritual*.

> i. Materially, we can trust that God will provide for the giving heart. The promise of Philippians 4:19 (*my God shall supply all your need according to His riches in glory by Christ Jesus*) is made in the context of the

generous hearts of the Philippians (Philippians 4:15-18). If we give to God, He will give to us materially.

ii. Spiritually, we can trust that God will reward the giving heart both now and in eternity. Jesus spoke to this in Matthew 19:29: *And everyone who has left houses or brothers or sisters or father or mother or wife or children or lands, for My name's sake, shall receive a hundredfold, and inherit eternal life.* Jesus obviously did not mean that we would receive a hundred houses if we gave up our house for Him any more than He meant we would receive a hundred wives if we gave one up for Him! But He did mean that we are *never* the losers when we give to God. The Lord can never be in debt to any man, and we should never be afraid of giving God "too much." Spiritually or materially, you can't out-give God.

iii. "This harvest should be understood both in terms of the spiritual reward of eternal life and also referring to the earthly blessings with which God honours the beneficent. Not only in heaven does God reward the well-doing of the godly, but in this world as well." (Calvin)

2. (7) Giving should come from a right heart.

So let each one give as he purposes in his heart, not grudgingly or of necessity; for God loves a cheerful giver.

a. **So let each one give**: Giving is for **each one**. Every Christian should be a giver. Because of small resources some cannot give *much* but it is still important that they give, and that they give with the right kind of heart.

b. **As he purposes in his own heart**: Giving should be motivated by the **purposes** of our **own heart**. It should never be coerced or manipulated. We should give because we *want* to give and because God has put it in our **own heart** to give.

i. This can also be said in the sense that our giving *reveals* the **purposes in [our] own heart**. If we say we love the Lord more than surfing, but spend all our money on surfboards and do not give as we should to the Lord's work, then the way we spend our money shows the **purposes** of our **own heart** more accurately than our words do. Jesus said it simply: *For where your treasure is, there your heart will be also.* (Matthew 6:21)

c. **Not grudging or of necessity**: God does not want our giving to be **grudging** (reluctantly, regretfully given with plenty of complaining) or **of necessity** (given because someone has made us or manipulated us into giving). This is more the spirit behind *taxation*, not Biblical giving.

i. "The Jews had in the temple *two chests* for alms; the one was of what was *necessary*, i.e. what the law required, the other was of the *free-will offerings.* To escape perdition some would *grudgingly*, give what *necessity* obliged them; others would give *cheerfully*, for the love of God, and through pity to the poor. Of the *first*, nothing is said; they simply did what the law required. Of the *second*, much is said; *God loves them* ... To these two sorts of alms in the temple the apostle most evidently alludes." (Clarke)

d. **For God loves a cheerful giver**: Instead of giving in a **grudging** way or out **of necessity**, God wants us to give *cheerfully*. The ancient Greek word for **cheerful** (*hilaros*, used only here in the New Testament) is the root for our English word *hilarious*. God wants us to give *happily* because that is how God Himself gives.

i. True giving *comes* from a happy heart, and it also *gives* us a happy heart. The English poet Carlyle said that when he was a boy, a beggar came to the door when his parents were gone. On a youthful impulse he rushed to his room, broke his piggy bank, and gave the beggar all the money. He said that never before or since had he known such sheer happiness as came to him in that moment of giving.

ii. Not all giving is **cheerful** giving. "Many gifts are thus given sorrowfully, where the giver is induced to give by a regard to public opinion, or by stress of conscience." (Hodge) In Acts 5:1-11, Ananias and Sapphira stand as examples of giving for the wrong reasons, not out of a cheerful heart.

iii. "It must be hilarious giving, giving out of the heart, because you love to give, not because you are bound to give." (Morgan)

iv. God is the ultimate **cheerful giver**. He *delights* to give to us. "It is not difficult to suggest why God delights in the cheerful giver. He himself is such a giver and desires to see this characteristic restored among those who were created in his image." (Kruse)

3. (8-9) The right kind of giving is always blessed.

And God *is* able to make all grace abound toward you, that you, always having all sufficiency in all *things*, may have an abundance for every good work. As it is written: "He has dispersed abroad, He has given to the poor; His righteousness endures forever."

a. **God is able to make all grace abound toward you**: As we give, we must be persuaded that **God is able** to reward our giving. Just as **God is able** to make the sowing of seed **abound** to a great harvest, so **God is able** to bless our giving.

i. Jesus taught that even the smallest gift, if given with the right heart, would not go without a reward: *And whoever gives one of these little ones only a cup of cold water in the name of a disciple, assuredly, I say to you, he shall by no means lose his reward.* (Matthew 10:42)

ii. In rewarding our giving, God does it with **all grace**. Our giving is rewarded in many different ways, materially and spiritually. Materially, God may bless our giving by promotions with better pay, unexpected gifts of money, or by making things last so we don't suffer the cost of replacing them. Spiritually, God may bless our giving by freeing our hearts from the tyranny of greed and materialism, by giving us a sense of blessing and happiness, or by storing up rich reward in heaven. There is no end to the ways we can be blessed when **God is able to make all grace abound toward** us.

b. **Always having all sufficiency in all things**: The ancient Greek word for **sufficiency** (*autarkeia*) may also be translated *contentment*. This is how the same word is used in 1 Timothy 6:6: *Now godliness with contentment is great gain*. God gives a special gift to the giving heart: **always . . . all** contentment **in all things**. That is a lot of **all**!

i. Materially speaking, how can someone **always** have **all** contentment **in all things**? By receiving this contentment God blesses the giving heart with.

ii. It's easy for many Christians to *say* they have this contentment; but whether they have it or not is often more truthfully known by their spending and shopping habits. How much of a place does shopping and buying have in your life? How does material loss affect your happiness? How happy do you get from having some material thing?

iii. When we live and act without contentment, we are trying to fill needs in our lives. It might be the need to be "somebody," the need to feel secure or cared for, or the need to have excitement and newness in our lives. Most people try to fulfill these needs with material things, but they can only really be met by a spiritual relationship with the God who made us.

iv. Barclay says of this ancient Greek word *autarkeia*: "By it they meant a complete *self-sufficiency*. They meant a frame of mind which was completely independent of all outward things, and which carried the secret of happiness within itself. Contentment never comes from the possession of external things." "The apostle useth many 'alls' on purpose to cross and confute our covetousness, who are apt to think we have never enough." (Trapp)

v. With this contentment, we can be the richest people in the world. A man might have the wealth of the richest man in the world, yet lack contentment. But if we have this contentment, it really does make us better off than the wealthiest people who don't have it.

c. **May have an abundance for every good work**: God blesses us materially and spiritually so that we will **have an abundance for every good work**. We are blessed so that we can be a blessing to others. God wants us to be *channels* of blessing, not *reservoirs* of blessing.

d. **His righteousness remains forever**: In the quotation from Psalm 112:9, Paul is not trying to say that generous giving *makes* us righteous but gives evidence of a right standing with God.

4. (10-11) Paul prays for blessing for the giving Corinthian Christians.

Now may He who supplies seed to the sower, and bread for food, supply and multiply the seed you have *sown* and increase the fruits of your righteousness, while *you are* enriched in everything for all liberality, which causes thanksgiving through us to God.

a. **May He who supplies seed to the sower, and bread for food**: Paul recognizes God as the great supplier. Whatever we have to give was first given to us by God.

i. "Our translators render it in the form of a prayer; which yet being the prayer of the apostle, put up in faith, doth virtually contain a promise both of a temporal and a spiritual increase." (Poole)

b. **Supply and multiply the seed you have sown**: Paul prays that God would **supply** resources to the Corinthian Christians so that they may give, and at the same time **multiply** what they give.

c. **Increase the fruits of your righteousness**: The giving of the Corinthian Christians (represented by **the seed you have sown**) will give a harvest, **the fruits of your righteousness**. Paul prays that God would **increase** these **fruits** that grow from their giving.

d. **While you are enriched in everything**: Paul prayed that the Corinthian Christians would be **enriched** by their giving, both materially and spiritually.

e. **For all liberality**: This is the reason why the Corinthian Christians should be **enriched in everything**. Not for their own riches or lavish lifestyles but **for all liberality** - that is, for all generous giving.

i. "No man ought to live to himself; the two great ends of every Christian's life ought to be, the glory of God, and the good of others, especially such as belong to the household of faith." (Poole)

f. **Which causes thanksgiving through us to God**: After all the giving is done, and **all liberality** is shown by the Corinthian Christians, the **thanksgiving** is directed **to God**.

> i. In his translation of the New Testament, J. B. Phillips carries the sense of this prayer: "He who gives the seed to the sower and turns that seed into bread to eat, will give you the seed of generosity to sow and, for harvest, the satisfying bread of good deeds done. The more you are enriched by God the more scope there will be for generous giving, and your gifts, administered through us, will mean that many will thank God."

5. (12-14) Four benefits of the giving from the Corinthian Christians.

For the administration of this service not only supplies the needs of the saints, but also is abounding through many thanksgivings to God, while, through the proof of this ministry, they glorify God for the obedience of your confession to the gospel of Christ, and for *your* liberal sharing with them and all *men*, and by their prayer for you, who long for you because of the exceeding grace of God in you.

a. **Not only supplies the needs of the saints**: First, on the most practical level, the giving of the Corinthian Christians will supply **the needs of the saints**. This is a good thing in and of itself, but their giving did far more than that.

b. **Many thanksgivings to God**: Secondly, their gifts also caused thanksgiving to God . They were giving more than money for food; they were giving people a reason to thank God.

c. **The obedience of your confession**: Third, the giving of the Corinthian Christians was evidence of God's work in them. When those in need received the gift, they would **glorify God for the obedience of your confession to the gospel of Christ, and for your liberal sharing**. The thanksgiving coming from the gift of the Corinthian Christians would be for more than the gift itself. They would also **glorify God** as they understood the gift meant **the obedience of your confession to the gospel of Christ**, and it meant the Corinthian Christians had hearts of **liberal sharing**.

> i. Paul puts it boldly. Giving among the Corinthian Christians was evidence of their **obedience** to their **confession to the gospel of Christ**. If a person does not have a generous heart, there is a sense in which they are not *obedient* to the **confession** of **the gospel of Christ**.

> ii. Others would also thank God because the gift from the Corinthian Christians will show that they have hearts of **liberal sharing**. This

meant God was really doing a work in the hearts of the Corinthian Christians, and that was something worth thanking God for.

iii. **Liberal sharing**: The ancient Greek word translated **sharing** is *koinania*. This is the same word used for the ideas of *fellowship* and *communion* - it means the sharing of things in common.

- When we share our lives, *koinania* is called *fellowship*

- When we share remembrance of Jesus' work for us through the Lord's Supper, *koinania* is called *communion*

- When we share our resources so none would be destitute, *koinania* is called **sharing**

d. **And by their prayer for you**: The fourth benefit from the gift of the Corinthian Christians was that it would prompt the Jerusalem Christians to pray for them. Paul expected that the Jerusalem Christians would pray for the Corinthian Christians. This is something that we can do when others give to us, and when we need their gifts. We can pray for them.

6. (15) Praise to God for the greatest gift.

Thanks *be* to God for His indescribable gift!

a. What is **His indescribable gift**? Some think it is the gift of salvation; others think it is the gift of Jesus Christ. Why not both? Salvation is given to us in Jesus Christ.

i. Paul wants to leave the discussion of giving by reminding us again that God is the greatest giver. He gives the **gift** beyond description: *For God so loved the world that He gave His only begotten Son, that whoever believes in Him should not perish but have everlasting life.* (John 3:16)

b. **Indescribable gift**: This means that Jesus is a **gift** and salvation is a **gift**. We do not earn it. We receive Jesus and we receive salvation exactly as we would receive a **gift**. If we earn it, it is not a **gift**.

c. **Indescribable gift**: This means that Jesus is an **indescribable gift**, and salvation is an **indescribable gift**. The glory of the gift of Jesus and the greatness of the gift of salvation cannot be adequately described.

i. Paul isn't saying that we *shouldn't* describe the gift of Jesus or the gift of salvation. He is simply saying that it is impossible to *adequately* describe the gift. It is beyond full description.

ii. "JESUS CHRIST, *the gift of God's love* to mankind, is an *unspeakable blessing*; no man can *conceive*, much less *declare*, how great this gift is; for these things the angels desire to look into. Therefore he may be well called the unspeakable gift, as he is the highest God ever gave or can give to man." (Clarke)

iii. "Ah, how many times have I, for one, spoken upon this gift during the last forty years! I have spoken of little else. I heard one who said, 'I suppose Spurgeon is preaching that old story over again.' Yes, that is what he is doing; and if he lives another twenty years, and you come here, it will be 'the old, old story' still, for there is nothing like it." (Spurgeon)

iv. "If you preach Christ, you will never run short. If you have preached ten thousand sermons about Christ, you have not left the shore; you are not out in the deep sea yet. Dive, my brother! With splendour of thought, plunge into the great mystery of free grace and dying love; and when you have dived the farthest, you will perceive that you are as far off the bottom as when you first touched the surface." (Spurgeon)

v. In fact, when Paul writes **His indescribable gift**, the ancient Greek word he uses for **indescribable** (*anekdiegetos*) is not found in any ancient writing before this time. Apparently, Paul made up the word to describe the indescribable.

d. **Thanks be to God**: This means God's **indescribable gift** should fill us with gratitude. If we really understand and appreciate the **indescribable gift** God gives us, our lives will be saturated with gratitude.

i. "Our affliction we scarcely ever forget; our mercies we scarcely ever remember! Our hearts are alive to *complaint*, but dead to *gratitude*. We have had ten thousand mercies for one judgment, and yet our complaints to our thanksgivings have been ten thousand to one! How is it that God endures this, and bears with us?" (Clarke)

e. **His indescribable gift**: How fitting for Paul to conclude these two chapters about giving with a focus on this! The best motivation for giving is always gratitude for the **indescribable gift** of God to us. God's **indescribable gift** is what inspires all true giving.

i. "The apostle concludeth this whole discourse about contributing to the relief of these poor members of Christ, who is the Author and Finisher of all grace . . . that without the influence of his grace they would, they could do nothing." (Poole)

2 Corinthians 10 - How To Judge An Apostle

A. Does Paul walk according to the flesh?

1. (1) Paul pleads with the Corinthians.

Now I, Paul, myself am pleading with you by the meekness and gentleness of Christ; who in presence *am* lowly among you, but being absent am bold toward you.

a. **Now I, Paul, myself am pleading with you**: Paul introduces this chapter with a change of tone. Some have even thought that 2 Corinthians 10 through 13 really make up a different letter that was added to the end of 2 Corinthians 1 through 9. This isn't likely, but it does show that Paul is changing gears as he ends the letter.

i. "Having now finished his directions and advices relative to the *collection for the poor*, he resumes his argument relative to the false apostle, who had gained considerable influence by representing St. Paul as despicable in his person, his ministry, and his influence." (Clarke)

b. **Pleading with you by the meekness and gentleness of Christ**: In these next few chapters, Paul will get a little "rough" with the Corinthian Christians. Yet he does it all in **the meekness and gentleness of Christ**.

c. **Who in presence am lowly among you, but being absent am bold toward you**: Here, Paul reveals a matter of great contention between him and the Corinthian Christians. They said that Paul seemed reserved in person but very bold in his letters.

i. The Corinthians criticized Paul as if he were a dog that barked loudly, but only at a distance. They accused him of backing down in any face-to-face confrontation.

d. How can the same person be **in presence lowly** and **bold toward you** at other times? Isn't this contradictory? It isn't a contradiction at all. Those who can't see that boldness and lowliness can be found in the same person don't know the life of Jesus very well.

2. (2) Paul hopes that the Corinthians will change their attitude towards him and his credentials as an apostle so that he may come to them in gentleness, not severity.

But I beg *you* that when I am present I may not be bold with that confidence by which I intend to be bold against some, who think of us as if we walked according to the flesh.

a. **I intend to be bold against some: Some** reminds us that we shouldn't think that *all* the Corinthian Christians had a bad opinion or Paul. It may have been merely a vocal minority.

b. **Who think of us as if walked according to the flesh**: This is another aspect of the accusations made against Paul by some of the Corinthian Christians. They said he was a man who **walked according to the flesh.**

i. He is accused of this because of the perceived contradiction between his gentleness and his severity.

c. In the following section, Paul will defend his apostolic authority. It is important to see how vital Paul's sense of apostolic authority was to him. Today, the idea of apostolic authority is cheapened by many of those who claim to be "apostles."

3. (3-6) Does Paul minister according to the flesh?

For though we walk in the flesh, we do not war according to the flesh. For the weapons of our warfare *are* not carnal but mighty in God for pulling down strongholds, casting down arguments and every high thing that exalts itself against the knowledge of God, bringing every thought into captivity to the obedience of Christ, and being ready to punish all disobedience when your obedience is fulfilled.

a. **For though we walk in the flesh**: Paul will admit that he walks according to the flesh in the sense that we all do. He is a flesh and blood human being, and he struggles with the same things the Corinthian Christians struggled with. However, Paul wants to make it clear that he does not **war according to the flesh.**

b. **For the weapons of our warfare are not carnal**: When Paul fought, his weapons were not material but spiritual, suited for spiritual war.

i. The **carnal** weapons Paul refuses were not material weapons such as swords and spears. The **carnal** weapons he renounced were the manipulative and deceitful ways his opponents used. Paul would not defend his apostolic credentials with **carnal** weapons others used.

ii. In Ephesians 6, Paul lists the spiritual weapons he used: the belt of truth, the breastplate of righteousness, the shoes of the gospel, the shield of faith, the helmet of salvation, and the sword of the Spirit. To rely on these weapons took faith in God instead of **carnal** methods. But truly, these weapons are **mighty in God for pulling down strongholds**.

iii. The Corinthian Christians tended to rely on and admire **carnal** weapons for the Christian battle:

- Instead of the belt of truth, they fought with manipulation

- Instead of the breastplate of righteousness, they fought with the image of success

- Instead of the shoes of the gospel, they fought with smooth words

- Instead of the shield of faith, they fought with the perception of power

- Instead of the helmet of salvation, they fought with lording over authority

- Instead of the sword of the Spirit, they fought with human schemes and programs

iv. Jesus relied on spiritual weapons when He fought for our salvation. Philippians 2:6-8 describes this: *who, being in the form of God, did not consider it robbery to be equal with God, but made Himself of no reputation, taking the form of a bondservant, and coming in the likeness of men. And being found in appearance as a man, He humbled Himself and became obedient to the point of death, even the death of the cross.* This kind of victory through humble obedience offended the Corinthian Christians because it seemed so "weak." The carnal, human way is to overpower, dominate, manipulate, and out-maneuver. The spiritual, Jesus way is to humble yourself, die to yourself, and let God show His resurrection power through you.

v. "Apart from a mighty awakening and revival in the church, we are fighting a losing battle because we are resisting on carnal levels." (Redpath)

vi. Our spiritual weapons are scorned by the world but feared by demonic powers. When we fight with true spiritual weapons, then no principality or power can stand against us. "As the spittle that comes out of a man's mouth slayeth serpents, so doth that which proceedeth out of the mouths of God's faithful ministers quell and kill evil imaginations, carnal reasonings, which are the legion of domestic devils, that hold near intelligence with the old serpent." (John Trapp)

c. **Pulling down strongholds: Strongholds** in this context are wrong thoughts and perceptions, contradicting the true knowledge of God and the nature of God. These **strongholds** are expressed in **arguments and every high thing that exalts itself against the knowledge of God**.

i. This reliance on carnal methods and the habit of carnal thinking is a true stronghold. It stubbornly sets down deep roots in the heart and mind, and it colors all of our actions and thinking. It is hard to let go of the thinking that values the things and ways of this world, but God's power really can break down these **strongholds**.

ii. In Paul's native land of Cilicia, some fifty years before he was born, Roman armies destroyed many rocky fortresses to defeat the pirates who had taken refuge in those strongholds. Perhaps Paul saw the ruins and thought of the battle needed to conquer those fortresses.

iii. Redpath writes of a practical way to battle with spiritual weapons and break down a stronghold: "When the thought comes and the person is reported to have said what he has said, and the unkindness has been passed over to us, and the criticism has been made, whereas carnality would say, 'Counterattack!' spirituality recognizes that nothing that any person could ever say about any one is really one hundredth part as bad as the truth if he only knew it. Therefore, we have no reason to counterattack, but one good reason to submit and to forget."

iv. Praise God, **strongholds** can be pulled down! Clarke recounts with wonder one stronghold pulled down in history: "In like manner the doctrines of the *reformation*, mighty through God, *pulled down* - demolished and *brought into captivity*, the whole papal system; and instead of *obedience to the pope*, the pretended vicar of God upon the earth, *obedience to Christ*, as the sole almighty Head of the Church, was established, particularly in Great Britain, where it continues to prevail. Hallelujah! The Lord God Omnipotent reigneth!" (Adam Clarke)

d. **Arguments and every high thing that exalts itself against the knowledge of God**: Carnal and worldly ways of thinking and doing are **arguments** against the mind and methods of God. They want to debate God, saying they have a better way. They exalt themselves **against the knowledge of God**. They think of themselves as smarter, more sophisticated, more effective, more powerful than God's ways. Carnal, worldly minds think they know more than God does!

i. We must remind ourselves that Paul speaks to carnal, worldly thinking *among Christians*. He isn't talking about the world here but the Corinthian Christians. They were the ones with the **strongholds** in their minds and hearts. They made the **arguments** against God's mind and methods. They held on to **every high thing that exalts itself against the knowledge of God**. We miss it entirely if we think the love of manipulation, the image of success, smooth words, the perception of power, lording over authority, and human schemes and programs are just problems among unbelievers. Paul dealt with this heart and mind in the church.

ii. "For nothing is more opposed to the spiritual wisdom of God than the wisdom of the flesh, and nothing more opposed to His grace than man's natural ability." (Calvin)

e. **Bringing every thought into captivity to the obedience of Christ**: To battle against this carnal way of thinking and doing, our *thoughts* must be *brought captive* and made obedient to Jesus.

i. When we start to think in this carnal way, we must stop our thoughts, take dominion over them in Jesus, and *not be conformed to this world, but be transformed by the renewing of your mind.* (Romans 12:2)

ii. Paul's first application is towards the carnal, worldly thinking of the Corinthian Christians that made them despise Paul and his "weakness," doubting his apostolic credentials. But Paul's principle has a much broader application. We are not helpless victims or recipients of our thoughts. We can choose to stop our thoughts and bring **every thought into captivity to the obedience of Christ**. Thoughts of lust, thoughts of anger, thoughts of fear, thoughts of greed, bitter thoughts, evil thoughts - they are part of **every thought** that may be and must be brought **into captivity to the obedience of Christ**.

iii. Someone might object: "I don't want my thoughts to be captive to anyone. I don't want my thoughts to be captive to Jesus. I want my thoughts to be free." This is wrong on at least two points. First, you belong to *someone*, and ultimately we either serve Jesus or Satan. Second, if you are a Christian, you are a *purchased possession of Jesus Christ*. You belong to Him. 1 Corinthians 6:19-20 puts it this way: *Or do you not know that your body is the temple of the Holy Spirit who is in you, whom you have from God, and you are not your own? For you were bought at a price; therefore glorify God in your body and in your spirit, which are God's.*

f. **And being ready to punish all disobedience**: Paul was ready to confront the Corinthian Christians and to pull down the strongholds among them if they would not do it themselves.

i. Many commentators think the phrase **to punish all disobedience** is taken from the Roman military court. Paul says, "We are all soldiers together in this battle, and I am ready to bring in some discipline among these troops."

ii. **When your obedience is fulfilled**: Paul sees no point in coming to confront disobedience until those who have obeyed Jesus have made up their mind to do so. He will give time for those who want to renounce carnal weapons to do so. Then he will come to punish the disobedience of those who will not renounce those carnal weapons.

iii. "Herein the apostle hath set a rule and a pattern to all churches, where are multitudes that walk disorderly; not to be too hasty in excommunicating them, but to proceed gradually; first using all fair means, and waiting with all patience, for the reducing them to their duty, who will by any gentle and fair means be reduced; and then revenging the honour and glory of God only upon such as will not be reclaimed." (Poole)

4. (7) The Corinthian Christians had a carnal reliance on outward appearances.

Do you look at things according to the outward appearance? If anyone is convinced in himself that he *is* Christ's, let him again consider this in himself, that just as he is Christ's, even so we *are* Christ's.

a. **Do you look at things according to the outward appearance?** Paul diagnoses the problem with the Corinthian troublemakers. They are looking only at the **outward** appearances, and by **outward** appearances, Paul was weak and unimpressive.

i. By **outward appearance**, it seems Paul was indeed unimpressive. This is a description of Paul from an early Christian writing, perhaps from about the year 200: "A man of small stature, with a bald head and crooked legs, in a good state of body, with eyebrows meeting and nose somewhat hooked." (Cited in Kruse) If this description of Paul is even remotely correct, he had nothing like magnetic good looks.

ii. "Since Paul excelled in none of those endowments which ordinarily win praise or reputation among the children of this world, he was despised as one of the common herd." (Calvin)

iii. But they knew Paul only on an outward, surface level. The people who criticized Paul and said that there were "two Pauls" - one reflected in his letters and one evident in person - really didn't know Paul except on a surface level.

b. **Just as he is Christ's, so we are Christ's**: Paul is saying, "If you claim to belong to Jesus, look at yourself. You may not be mighty in outward appearance, yet you belong to Jesus. Well, **so we are Christ's** as well."

2 Corinthians 11 - Paul's "Foolish Boasting"

A. Why Paul defends his credentials.

1. (1) Introduction: Please bear with me!

Oh, that you would bear with me in a little folly; and indeed you do bear with me.

a. **Oh, that you would bear with me in a little folly**: Paul does not call the defense of his apostleship **folly** because it is stupid or nonsense. He calls it **folly** because he does it reluctantly, knowing his time and effort could be spent on far better things. He calls it **folly** because he knows that the things he believed to be honorable about his apostleship would be regarded as foolish by some of the Corinthian Christians.

b. **And indeed you do bear with me**: One might ask, "Paul, if you think this is **a little folly**, why bother with it at all?" Yet it is worth it, for the reasons Paul will explain in the following passage.

2. (2-4) Why Paul's apostolic credentials are important.

For I am jealous for you with godly jealousy. For I have betrothed you to one husband, that I may present *you as* a chaste virgin to Christ. But I fear, lest somehow, as the serpent deceived Eve by his craftiness, so your minds may be corrupted from the simplicity that is in Christ. For if he who comes preaches another Jesus whom we have not preached, or *if* you receive a different spirit which you have not received, or a different gospel which you have not accepted; you may well put up with it!

a. **For I am jealous for you with godly jealousy**: It is important that the Corinthian Christians understand and trust Paul's apostolic credentials because Paul is **jealous** with a **godly jealousy** for their hearts. Paul's **godly jealousy** is a good thing, and he will be offended if the Corinthians are seduced by a false understanding of what being an apostle is all about.

i. Human jealousy is a vice but the Lord said, *I, the LORD your God, am a jealous God.* (Exodus 20:5) "God's jealousy is love in action. He refuses to share the human heart with any rival, not because He is selfish and wants us all for Himself, but because He knows that upon that loyalty to Him depends our very moral life . . . God is not jealous *of* us: He is jealous *for* us." (Redpath in *Law and Liberty*) Sharing God's jealousy for His people is a virtue.

ii. "God's jealousy, therefore, is a concern for the holiness, integrity, purity of ethics, and Christian standards for His people. Because of this, He will refuse to brook a rival in our affections for Him, not because of a selfish greed which wishes us all for His own possession, but simply because He knows that His great purpose for us of purity and holiness of life depends on our personal surrender and submission to His purpose." (Redpath)

b. **For I have betrothed you to one husband, that I may present you as a chaste virgin to Christ**: It is important that the Corinthian Christians understand and trust Paul's apostolic credentials because Paul is like the friend of the groom, who watches out for the bride in the period between the betrothal and the wedding.

i. Paul considers himself the friend of Jesus the bridegroom, and he will do his best to present the bride **as a chaste virgin to Christ** on the "wedding day" - when the Corinthian Christians one day stand before Jesus.

ii. In the Jewish culture of that day, the *friend of the bridegroom* (mentioned also in John 3:29) had an important job. "To procure a husband for the virgin, to guard her, and to bear testimony to her corporeal and marital endowments; and it was upon this testimony of this friend that the bridegroom chose his bride. He was the *intercnuncio* between her and her spouse elect; carrying all messages from her to him, and from him to her: for before marriage you women were strictly guarded at home with their parents or friends." Also, the *friend of the bridegroom* was called upon, if necessary, "To vindicate the character of the bride." (Clarke)

iii. Remember also that the time of betrothal wasn't taken lightly in Paul's culture. If someone was unfaithful during the betrothal period, it was considered adultery, and a betrothal could only be broken by divorce.

iv. Anytime we give our hearts to something other than God, we are committing "spiritual adultery" during the period of our betrothal.

c. **But I fear . . . your minds may be corrupted from the simplicity that is in Christ**: It is important that the Corinthian Christians understand and trust Paul's apostolic credentials because Paul knows the subtle nature of Satan's deceptions.

i. Bottom line, the Corinthian Christians didn't admire Paul's apostolic credentials because they thought in a worldly way, not having the mind of Jesus. They didn't like Paul's apparent weakness and unimpressive appearance. This was an important point because Paul's apparent weakness was shared by Jesus *who, being in the form of God, did not consider it robbery to be equal with God, but made Himself of no reputation, taking the form of a bondservant, and coming in the likeness of men. And being found in appearance as a man, He humbled Himself and became obedient to the point of death, even the death of the cross.* (Philippians 2:6-8) It wasn't only the apostolic credentials of Paul that were under attack; the very nature of Jesus was attacked.

ii. **As the serpent deceived Eve by his craftiness**: Paul understood that Satan's deception of Eve in the Garden of Eden (Genesis 3:1-5) is a good example of Satan's deceptive tactics. His lie to Eve (*You will not surely die*) was surrounded by half-truths and enticing deception. The Corinthian Christians were challenged by the deception of "trimuphalism" because it was wrapped in the truth of the triumphant life we can live in Jesus Christ.

iii. Satan's lie to Eve recalls lines from Tennyson:

> *"A lie that is all of a lie can be met with and fought outright;*
> *But a lie that is partly the truth is a harder matter to fight."*

d. **For if he who comes preaches another Jesus**: It is important that the Corinthian Christians understand and trust Paul's apostolic credentials because Paul knows they are attracted to the false apostles who preach **another Jesus**.

i. The troublemakers among the Corinthian Christians who stirred up contention against Paul didn't only attack Paul; they also attacked the true Jesus by preaching **another Jesus**. Who was this "other Jesus?" Because of the way the Corinthian Christians despised Paul's image of weakness and unimpressive appearance, the "other Jesus" was probably one who knew no weakness, persecution, humiliation, suffering, or death. A "super Jesus" is **another Jesus**, not the real Jesus, and **another Jesus** cannot save.

ii. **Whom we have not preached . . . a different spirit . . . or a different gospel**: Paul warned the Galatians against receiving another Jesus. *But even if we, or an angel from heaven, preach any other gospel to you* *than what we have preached to you, let him be accursed. As we have said before, so now I say again, if anyone preaches any other gospel to you than what you have received, let him be accursed.* (Galatians 1:8-9)

e. **If He who comes**: An *apostle* is "one who is sent." These troublemakers were the exact opposite of apostles. One could say of them, "**He who comes**." Of an apostle, one could say "*one who is sent*" by God. These false apostles had simply *come*; they were not really sent by God.

f. **You may well put up with it**: The problem wasn't so much that these false teachers had come among the Christians in Corinth. The problem was that the Corinthian Christians put up with them.

> i. The church has the same problem today. It is not surprising that there are false teachers in the church today; the problem is that the church puts up with them and embraces them. Christians of this generation, like Christians of many generations, will have to answer to Jesus for their lack of discernment when it comes to the false teachers and leaders accepted and embraced by the church.

3. (5-9) Paul's "foolish" humility.

For I consider that I am not at all inferior to the most eminent apostles. Even though *I am* untrained in speech, yet *I am* not in knowledge. But we have been thoroughly manifested among you in all things. Did I commit sin in humbling myself that you might be exalted, because I preached the gospel of God to you free of charge? I robbed other churches, taking wages *from them* to minister to you. And when I was present with you, and in need, I was a burden to no one, for what I lacked the brethren who came from Macedonia supplied. And in everything I kept myself from being burdensome to you, and so I will keep *myself*.

a. **For I consider that I am not at all inferior to the most eminent apostles**: Paul here compares himself to some he refers to as **the most eminent apostles**. Apparently, these were apostles that the Corinthian Christians preferred over Paul.

> i. Commentators warmly debate the identity of these **most eminent apostles**. Some think they were other prominent apostles such as Peter or Apollos (as mentioned in 1 Corinthians 1:12). This isn't likely. Probably, Paul speaks sarcastically of the false apostles who claimed to be superior to Paul.

> ii. In the original language, the idea behind the phrase **most eminent apostles** is "extra-super apostles." Paul probably writes sarcastically

in reference to those who thought of and promoted themselves as "super-duper apostles."

iii. **I am not at all inferior:** Whoever these **most eminent apostles** are, Paul will not claim to be *less* than they. Later Paul will explain how he (in an unlikely way) is *greater* than these supposed **most eminent apostles**.

b. **Even though I am untrained in speech:** Paul, according to the standards of Greek rhetoric, was **untrained in speech.** In Paul's day, the ability to speak in a polished, sophisticated, entertaining way was popular. Others (such as **the most eminent apostles** the Corinthian Christians loved so much) were able to speak in this manner, but Paul was either unable or unwilling to preach in this way. It didn't matter to Paul because he wasn't concerned with meeting people's standards for a "polished" or "entertaining" speaker; he was concerned with faithfully preaching the gospel.

i. A story is told about a dinner party where the guests were expected to stand after the meal and recite something for the group. A famous actor was present, and he recited the twenty-third Psalm with great dramatic flair and emotion, and sat down to great applause. Then a very simple man got up and began to recite the same Psalm. He wasn't very eloquent, so at first people thought it was a little funny. But his presentation was straight from his heart, so when he finished the group sat in respectful silence. It was obvious that the simple man's presentation was more powerful than the actor's, and afterwards the actor told him: "I know the Psalm, but you know the Shepherd."

ii. That was the difference between the preaching of Paul and the preaching of **the most eminent apostles.** Paul didn't have all the polish and panache of a great speaker, but he knew God, and thus preached the gospel with power.

c. **But we have been thoroughly manifested among you in all things**: Paul couldn't - or wouldn't - give the Corinthian Christians the polished and entertaining preaching they wanted, but he did give them *himself.* He **thoroughly manifested** himself among the Corinthian Christians **in all things**. He wasn't a polished speaker (according to the standards of his day), but he was an honest and transparent speaker.

d. **Did I commit sin in humbling myself . . . because I preached the gospel of God to you free of charge?** In the culture of that day, if a public speaker didn't take money for his speaking he was often disregarded as a poor speaker, with worthless teaching. Many people thought of someone who charged no speaking fee as strictly an amateur. But Paul didn't care about the opinion of others when it came to his heart for preaching the gospel without being accused of doing it for money.

i. **Did I commit sin?** This shows Paul at his most ironic. The Corinthian Christians who despised Paul were so worldly in their thinking they actually thought Paul might be in **sin** because he **preached the gospel of God to you free of charge!**

e. **I robbed other churches, taking wages from them to minister to you**: The word Paul used for **robbed** is strong. In classical Greek, this word was used for stripping a dead soldier of his armor.

i. Paul refers to the fact that he received support from Christians in other cities during his time in Corinth. He could say he **robbed** those other churches in the sense that by right, the Corinthian Christians should have supported him when he ministered to their spiritual needs (1 Corinthian 9:4-11). Instead, Paul **was a burden to no one** among the Corinthian Christians.

ii. **For what I lacked the brethren who came from Macedonia supplied**: The **other churches** Paul "robbed" were in the region of **Macedonia**, including the Philippian church. Paul thanked them for their generosity in Philippians 4:14-18.

4. (10-15) Paul against the false apostles.

As the truth of Christ is in me, no one shall stop me from this boasting in the regions of Achaia. Why? Because I do not love you? God knows! But what I do, I will also continue to do, that I may cut off the opportunity from those who desire an opportunity to be regarded just as we are in the things of which they boast. For such *are* false apostles, deceitful workers, transforming themselves into apostles of Christ. And no wonder! For Satan himself transforms himself into an angel of light. Therefore *it is* no great thing if his ministers also transform themselves into ministers of righteousness, whose end will be according to their works.

a. **No one shall stop me from this boasting**: As a true apostle, Paul could "boast" that he took no money and that he was more interested in the integrity of the message than in his own needs.

b. **Why? Because I do not love you? God knows!** Paul's **boasting** in his weakness and unimpressive image was an embarrassment to the Corinthian Christians. Why did he embarrass them this way? It was only because he loved them and would find a way to bring them back from their worldly thinking.

c. **I will continue to do, that I may cut off the opportunity from those who desire an opportunity to be regarded just as we are**: Paul wanted to expose these *most eminent apostles* as frauds. If it took biting sarcasm or embarrassing the Corinthian Christians to expose them, Paul would use those tools.

d. **For such are false apostles, deceitful workers, transforming themselves into apostles of Christ**: Here Paul becomes even more direct. Without sarcasm, he plainly calls his detractors in Corinth (or at least the leaders among them) **false apostles** and **deceitful workers**.

> i. Few modern Christians want to deal with the fact that there are still **false apostles** and **deceitful workers** among Christians. Nevertheless, they were clearly there in Paul's day, and they remain to this day.

> ii. **False apostles** are those who are **transforming themselves into apostles of Christ**. In fact, no one can **transform themselves** into a true apostle of Jesus; it is only a calling from God. "They were never apostles of Christ, only they put themselves into such a shape and form, that they might have more advantage to deceive." (Poole) As Paul will explain in the following sentence, those who *transform themselves* are more like Satan than they are like God.

e. **For Satan himself transforms himself into an angel of light. Therefore it is no great thing if his ministers also transform themselves into ministers of righteousness**: Even as Satan may appear as an **angel of light**, so false apostles may have a "good" appearance. Paul is showing the Corinthian Christians how foolish it is to rely on image and outward appearances.

> i. It is so easy for all people, including Christians, to be taken in by image and outward appearances. Many will only recognize evil if it openly declares itself as evil. But this approach will end up embracing **Satan himself**, who **transforms himself into an angel of light**. If Satan were to appear before a human audience, they would be strongly tempted to worship him as a creature of almost divine beauty. He would be regarded as **an angel of light**.

> ii. Even so, it is foolish for the Corinthian Christians - or us today - to be taken in by image and outward appearances.

> iii. Hughes rightly notes that in today's church, "an individual has only to make the most preposterous claims for himself in order to gain an enthusiastic and undiscerning following."

> iv. "It is generally said that Satan has *three forms* under which he tempts men: 1. The *subtle serpent*. 2. The *roaring lion*. 3. The *angel of light*. He often, as the *angel of light*, persuades men to do things under the *name of religion*, which are subversive of it. Hence all the *persecutions, faggots,* and *fires* of a certain Church, under pretence of keeping *heresy* out of

the Church; and hence all the *horrors* and *infernalities* of the *inquisition*. In the form of heathen persecution, like a *lion* he has ravaged the heritage of the Lord. And by means of our *senses* and *passions*, as the *subtle serpent*, he is frequently deceiving us, so that often the *workings* of *corrupt nature* are mistaken for the *operations* of the *Spirit of God*." (Clarke)

f. **According to their works**: This is the terrible condemnation reserved for these false apostles - to be judged **according to their works**.

B. Paul's credentials as a "foolish" apostle.

1. (16-21) Fools and boasting.

I say again, let no one think me a fool. If otherwise, at least receive me as a fool, that I also may boast a little. What I speak, I speak not according to the Lord, but as it were, foolishly, in this confidence of boasting. Seeing that many boast according to the flesh, I also will boast. For you put up with fools gladly, since you *yourselves* are wise! For you put up with it if one brings you into bondage, if one devours *you*, if one takes *from you*, if one exalts himself, if one strikes you on the face. To *our* shame, I say that we were too weak for that! But in whatever anyone is bold; I speak foolishly; I am bold also.

a. **Let no one think me a fool . . . I also may boast a little**: It is easy to sense both Paul's sarcasm and his hesitancy to promote himself. He would rather talk about Jesus, but that message is hindered by the Corinthians' disregard of Paul's credentials as a true apostle, a true representative of Jesus.

i. Paul is not like the "real" fools who boast of their credentials. This will become evident when Paul starts stating his credentials as a true apostle.

b. **What I speak, I speak not according to the Lord, but as it were, foolishly**: Paul speaks **not according to the Lord** in the sense that his defense of his credentials focuses on himself. Paul didn't like to talk about himself. He was happy to write *for we do not preach ourselves, but Christ Jesus the Lord* (2 Corinthians 4:5).

i. Paul feels forced into writing about himself: **Seeing that many boast according to the flesh, I also will boast**. But Paul's boasting will be nothing like the boasting of the **many** who **boast according to the flesh**.

c. **For you put up with fools gladly, since you yourselves are wise!** Again, Paul uses biting sarcasm. If the Corinthian Christians are **wise** enough to put up with so many fools, surely they can listen to Paul for a while!

d. **For you put up with it if one brings you into bondage**: Like many of the deceived today, the Corinthian Christians would put up with abuse from "super apostles," thinking that it is somehow spiritual to endure such **bondage**.

> i. The **bondage** Paul speaks of may indicate that these false apostles were legalists, trying to put people under the bondage of the Law. However, it is just as likely that the **bondage** Paul refers to is the personal domination and authority the *most eminent apostles* held over others. The emphasis on image and outward appearance is often coupled with an authoritarian approach to leadership, and this probably explains the **bondage** Paul refers to.

e. **If one devours you, if one takes from you, if one exalts himself, if one strikes you on the face**: The Corinthian Christians were so taken with their "super apostles" they would accept all kind of ill treatment from them. They were so impressed with the image of authority and power of the "super apostles," they meekly submitted to this kind of treatment.

> i. Would the Corinthian Christians even accept it **if one strikes you on the face**? They probably would because it wasn't uncommon for religious authorities in that day (outside of Jesus' true ministers) to command that those people they considered to be ungodly to actually be struck in the face (Acts 23:2, 1 Timothy 3:3).

> ii. Sadly, many people are more comfortable with authoritarian "super apostles" than they are with the freedom that is open to them in Jesus.

f. **To our shame, I say that we were too weak for that!** Paul continues the sarcasm, confessing that he is too "weak" to abuse his sheep the way the "super apostles" do. Guilty as charged!

g. **But in whatever anyone is bold - I speak foolishly - I am bold also**: The *most eminent apostles* were **bold** in proclaiming their greatness. So, Paul will be **bold also** but in doing so, he will **speak foolishly**. The rest of the chapter contains Paul's "foolish boasting" about the things that prove him to be a true apostle.

2. (22-33) Paul's apostolic credentials.

Are they Hebrews? So *am* I. Are they Israelites? So *am* I. Are they the seed of Abraham? So *am* I. Are they ministers of Christ?; I speak as a fool; I *am* more: in labors more abundant, in stripes above measure, in prisons more frequently, in deaths often. From the Jews five times I received forty *stripes* minus one. Three times I was beaten with rods; once I was stoned; three times I was shipwrecked; a night and a day I have been in the deep; *in* journeys often, *in* perils of waters, *in* perils of

robbers, *in* perils of *my own* countrymen, *in* perils of the Gentiles, *in* perils in the city, *in* perils in the wilderness, *in* perils in the sea, *in* perils among false brethren; in weariness and toil, in sleeplessness often, in hunger and thirst, in fastings often, in cold and nakedness; besides the other things, what comes upon me daily: my deep concern for all the churches. Who is weak, and I am not weak? Who is made to stumble, and I do not burn with indignation? If I must boast, I will boast in the things which concern my infirmity. The God and Father of our Lord Jesus Christ, who is blessed forever, knows that I am not lying. In Damascus the governor, under Aretas the king, was guarding the city of the Damascenes with a garrison, desiring to arrest me; but I was let down in a basket through a window in the wall, and escaped from his hands.

a. **Are they Hebrews? So am I:** Paul's human ancestry was more than enough to qualify him as an apostle. Not only was he **the seed of Abraham,** he was also of the **Israelites.** Not only was he of the **Israelites,** he was of the **Hebrews,** meaning he was a Jew of Judean descent, as opposed to Jews who were born from people coming from areas far from Judea.

i. Paul grew up in Tarsus of Cilicia (Acts 21:39), but this apparently means his parents were Judean Jews who moved to Tarsus either before or after Paul was born.

ii. Paul knows very well that his blood ancestry does not make him an apostle or a servant of Jesus, but many of the *most eminent apostles* either said or implied that it was important. Knowing the silliness of this, Paul prefaced his remarks here with "**I speak foolishly.**" Yet, to make a point (to expose the foolishness of the *most eminent apostles* and to glorify the nature of Jesus), he will continue.

b. **Are they ministers of Christ? - I speak as a fool - I am more:** The *most eminent apostles* claimed to be **ministers of Christ.** When they used this term, it probably sounded like an honored, privileged title. As for Paul, he will claim also to be among the **ministers of Christ,** but he will explain that he means something far different from what the *most eminent apostles* meant.

i. *Minister* comes from the ancient Greek word *diakonos,* which describes a humble servant or a menial worker. The *most eminent apostles* had inflated the idea of *minister* to make it a title of exaltation and privilege. Paul had no problem with the title *minister,* but he had a big problem with the understanding of the title promoted by the *most eminent apostles* and received by the Corinthian Christians. In the following section, Paul explains what qualifies him to be called a *minister of Christ.* We should expect it to be rather different from what the *most eminent apostles* would claim as their qualifications.

c. **In labors more abundant**: "I am a minister of Christ because I work harder than any of the other apostles for Jesus' sake." Paul said this even more explicitly in 1 Corinthians 15:10: *I labored more abundantly than they all.*

> i. In contrast, the *most eminent apostles* saw being a minister of Christ as a matter of *privilege.* In their minds, the more of a minister you were, the less you should have to work and the more others should serve you.

d. **In stripes above measure**: "I am a minister of Christ because I have been beaten many times for Jesus' sake." Paul received beatings from both the Jews (**five times I received forty stripes minus one**) and the Romans (**three times I beaten with rods**).

> i. Deuteronomy 25:3 says: *Forty blows he may give him and no more, lest he should exceed this and beat him with many blows above these, and your brother be humiliated in your sight.* Accordingly, the Rabbis restricted the number of stripes you could give to 39 (**forty stripes minus one**). They did this not out of mercy, but they feared that there might be a miscount and forty stripes would be exceeded by accident.

> ii. An ancient Jewish writing describes the procedure for receiving **stripes** in a Jewish court: "The two hands of the criminal are bound to a post, and then the servant of the synagogue either pulls or tears off his clothes till he leaves his breast and shoulders bare. A stone or block is placed behind him on which the servant stands; he holds in his hands a scourge made of leather, divided into four tails. He who scourges lays one third on the criminal's *breast,* another third on his *right shoulder,* and another third on his *left.* The man who receives the punishment is neither *sitting* nor *standing,* but all the while *stooping;* and the man smites with all his strength, with one hand." (Mishna, fol. 22, 2; cited in Clarke)

e. **In prisons more frequently**: "I am a minister of Christ because I have spent a lot of time in prison for Jesus' sake." Paul speaks of being in prison several times, even though Acts only tells us of one instance up to the time he wrote 2 Corinthians (in Philippi, Acts 16:20-24). This reminds us that as wonderful as the book of Acts is, it is an incomplete record.

f. **In deaths often**: "I am a minister of Christ because I have been close to death many times for Jesus' sake." We know Paul was close to death when an angry crowd tried to execute him by stoning in Lystra (Acts 14:19), but there were many other times as well.

i. The incident in Lystra (recorded in Acts 14:19) must be what Paul refers to when he says **once I was stoned.**

g. **Three times I was shipwrecked; a night and a day I have been in the deep; in journeys often, in perils:** "I am a minister of Christ because I have traveled many miles for Jesus' sake and have endured many hardships traveling for Jesus' sake." In the modern world, a busy travel schedule can be hard on anyone. Think of what it was like in the ancient world!

i. Through the book of Acts, we read of no less than 18 journeys Paul took by ship, with half of them occurring before the writing of 2 Corinthians. Since the book of Acts is an incomplete record, there were many more in addition to this. Some historians have said that there is no other man in the ancient world who is recorded to have traveled as extensively as Paul did.

h. **In perils of waters, in perils of robbers, in perils of my own countrymen, in perils of the Gentiles, in perils in the city, in perils in the wilderness, in perils in the sea, in perils among false brethren; in weariness and toil, in sleeplessness often, in hunger and thirst, in fastings often, in cold and nakedness:** "I am a minister of Christ because I have endured many perils and many discomforts for Jesus' sake."

i. All these **perils** simply add up to a hard, stress-filled life:

- **In perils of waters:** This refers to the great dangers Paul faced in crossing rivers as he traveled

- **In perils of robbers:** One of the worst dangers of travel in the ancient world were muggers ready to rob isolated travelers in the middle of nowhere (as Jesus illustrated in Luke 10:30)

- **In perils in the city:** Paul experienced many hostile mobs in the cities where he preached (Acts 13:50, 14:5, 14:19, 16:19, and so forth)

- **In perils in the wilderness:** In his travels, Paul spent many dangerous days and nights **in the wilderness**

- **In perils in the sea:** This refers to Paul's many shipwrecks and difficulties when traveling by sea

- **In perils among false brethren:** Paul had the danger of those who said they were brothers and his friends, but were **false brethren** instead (2 Timothy 4:14 is a later example)

ii. **In weariness and toil, in sleeplessness often, in hunger and thirst, in fastings often, in cold and nakedness:** In our modern world, we are isolated from so many of the difficulties Paul faced. We can get water and food and warmth so much more easily than Paul ever could. Paul simply *lived a hard life* as a missionary, traveling and preaching the gospel.

iii. It wasn't the mere fact of a hard life that made Paul a true minister of Christ. Many people have hard lives but are in no way servants of Jesus. But for Paul, all these perils and hardships were *freely chosen* because he could have lived differently if he wanted to. But he didn't want to. He wanted to serve Jesus, and if these hardships were part of serving Jesus, he would accept them.

iv. How could the man who lived this life possibly be *happy*? Because he had died to himself! Because Paul could say, *I have been crucified with Christ; it is no longer I who live, but Christ lives in me; and the life which I now live in the flesh I live by faith in the Son of God, who loved me and gave Himself for me.* (Galatians 2:20) Because of this, Paul could practice what he preached when he wrote: *we also glory in tribulations* (Romans 5:3). This wasn't just "spiritual talk" from Paul; he really lived it. Paul could say and mean what he wrote earlier in 2 Corinthians 4:17-18: *For our light affliction, which is but for a moment, is working for us a far more exceeding and eternal weight of glory, while we do not look at the things which are seen, but at the things which are not seen. For the things which are seen are temporary, but the things which are not seen are eternal.*

v. The *most eminent apostles*, and the Christian Corinthians who had bought into their worldly lies, must think Paul is *crazy* at this point. They found nothing to boast about in these hardships Paul gloried in. For them such hardships said, "God is not with me. I'm a loser. I'm weak. I'm not happy. My life is too hard." They could only glory in the *image* of power and the appearance of success. If they did not have that image, they felt God was against them. They thought this way because their thinking was worldly, instead of having the mind of Jesus as reflected in Philippians 2:5-11.

vi. "Such is the price that Paul paid. How does that react upon you? Do you congratulate yourself that you have escaped it? One week of such living and we would be done, but Paul went through it for a lifetime and gloried in his infirmities." (Redpath)

vii. The **perils** of Paul's life were really plenty enough to kill any man, but nothing or no one could kill him until God finished His purpose for Paul on this earth.

i. **Besides the other things, what comes upon me daily: my deep concern for all the churches**: In addition to all the stressful **perils** Paul previously mentioned, he lived **daily** with another burden. Paul lived with a **deep concern for all the churches**.

    i. The **perils** Paul mentioned were not everyday occurrences, but his **deep concern for all the churches** never left him. Paul's burdens were not only physical, but they were also emotional.

    ii. **Who is weak, and I am not weak? Who is made to stumble, and I do not burn with indignation?** Paul's **deep concern** was not for himself. It was for others - for the **weak** and those **made to stumble**. Paul had many burdens, but few of them were for himself. He, like Jesus, was truly an others-centered person.

    iii. Redpath on **what comes upon me daily**: "I could not possibly convey to you adequately in the English language the force of that statement. I tried to picture it in terms of being smothered under a blanket, or by being attacked and crushed by some great animal, for he could not have used a stronger word when he said, in effect, 'That which bears me down, that which is upon me as an intolerable load, that which is a burden, that which is something that I can never shake off day or night. It is with me always. I have no vacation for it ever. It is upon me daily. The care, the compassion, the concern of all the churches.' "

    iv. Paul's **deep concern** was not a "faithless fussiness." "This anxiety was based not only on disturbing reports which came to his ears, but on his knowledge of the savage subtlety of the enemy of souls who, he realized, would stop at nothing in his attempts to overthrow the work of the gospel." (Hughes)

j. **If I must boast, I will boast in the things which concern my infirmity**: What is Paul's boast? What are his credentials as an apostle? Only his scars, **the things which concern my infirmity**. The **infirmity** Paul refers to may be a specific illness or weakness; more likely, it is the life of hardship and stress he lived as a whole.

    i. The *false apostles*, those *most eminent apostles*, would never dream of boasting in such things. They thought any **infirmity** made one look weak and far from God. Despite that, Paul did not care if it looked foolish in the eyes of the world or those in the church who thought like the world. Paul lived with an eternal perspective, not a worldly perspective.

    ii. "I will not boast of my *natural* or *acquired powers*; neither in what *God* has done by me; but rather in what I have *suffered* for *him*." (Clarke)

k. **The God and Father of our Lord Jesus Christ, who is blessed forever, knows that I am not lying**: Paul recognizes that what he just wrote may seem incredible to some, and some may doubt Paul actually lived such hardship. Probably even more doubted that Paul could actually *boast* of such hardship. So Paul uses strong language to declare God is his witness that he tells the truth.

i. " 'God knoweth.' He knows what? Knows all the suffering, knows all the trial, knows all the facts, which he has already referred to, that he is led everywhere in triumph all the way. 'God knoweth.' That is the secret of his deepest boasting." (Morgan)

l. **In Damascus . . . I was let down in a basket through a window**: This was perhaps the first real peril or hardship Paul faced for Jesus' sake (Acts 9:23-25). He thinks way back to this beginning event, perhaps thinking that his escape from Damascus was his "apprenticeship in persecution." It is as if he says, "This is how my ministry began and this is how it continues."

i. Hughes says of this Damascus escape, "it was an event which emphasized, at the very beginning of his ministry, his own abject weakness and frailty."

ii. It illustrates with power the contrast between *Saul of Tarsus* and *Paul the Apostle*. Saul of Tarsus traveled to Damascus full of man's power and authority, directed against God's people. Paul the Apostle left Damascus humbly in a basket. Is there anything more descriptive of weakness than being let down in a basket over a wall? "Could we thing of anything more likely to rob a man of any sense of dignity than that?" (Morgan)

iii. The reference to **Aretas the king** dates Paul's escape from Damascus between 37 and 39 A.D. Taking into account the three years mentioned in Galatians 1:18, and that this incident happened at the end of those three years, we can surmise that Paul was converted sometime between 34 and 36 A.D.

2 Corinthians 12 - The Strength of Grace
in Weakness

A. Paul's vision and its legacy in his life.

1. (1-6) Paul reluctantly describes his vision.

It is doubtless not profitable for me to boast. I will come to visions and revelations of the Lord: I know a man in Christ who fourteen years ago; whether in the body I do not know, or whether out of the body I do not know, God knows; such a one was caught up to the third heaven. And I know such a man; whether in the body or out of the body I do not know, God knows; how he was caught up into Paradise and heard inexpressible words, which it is not lawful for a man to utter. Of such a one I will boast; yet of myself I will not boast, except in my infirmities. For though I might desire to boast, I will not be a fool; for I will speak the truth. But I refrain, lest anyone should think of me above what he sees me *to be* or hears from me.

a. **I will come to visions and revelations of the Lord**: The "super apostles" among the Corinthian Christians no doubt claimed many spectacular spiritual experiences, such as **visions and revelations of the Lord**. Paul has "reluctantly boasted" since the last chapter, so now he will boast of his own **visions and revelations of the Lord**.

i. Paul's reluctance is expressed in the opening words of this chapter: **It is doubtless not profitable for me to boast**. Paul is tired of writing about himself! He would rather write about Jesus, but the worldly thinking that made the Corinthian Christians think little of Paul also made them think little of Jesus, even if they couldn't perceive it.

b. **Visions and revelation**: Whether they concern angels, Jesus, heaven, or other things, these things are more common in the New Testament than we might think.

- Zechariah, the father of John the Baptist, had a vision of an angel (Luke 1:8-23)

- Jesus' transfiguration is described as a vision for the disciples (Matthew 17:9)

- The women who came to visit Jesus' tomb had a vision of angels (Luke 24:22-24)

- Stephen saw a vision of Jesus at his death (Acts 7:55-56)

- Ananias experienced a vision telling him to go to Saul (Acts 9:10)

- Peter had a vision of the clean and unclean animals (Acts 10:17-19 and 11:5)

- Peter had a vision of an angel at his release from prison (Acts 12:9)

- John had many visions on Patmos (Revelation 1:1)

- Paul had a revelation of Jesus on the road to Damascus (Acts 22:6-11 and 26:12-20)

- Paul had a vision of a man from Macedonia, asking him to come to that region to help (Acts 16:9-10)

- Paul had an encouraging vision while in Corinth (Acts 18:9-11)

- Paul had a vision of an angel on the ship that was about to be wrecked (Acts 27:23-25)

i. So we should not be surprised if God should speak to us through some type of **visions and revelations of the Lord**. But we do understand that such experiences are *subjective* and prone to misunderstanding and misapplication. In addition, whatever real benefits there are to **visions and revelations of the Lord**, they are almost always limited to the person who receives the **visions and revelations**. We should be rather cautious when someone reports a vision or revelation they have regarding us.

ii. "How often people have wanted to tell me about their visions! I am always suspicious. I want to know what they had for supper the night before! If people have visions of this sort they are silent about them." (Morgan)

c. **I know a man in Christ**: Paul describes this experience in the third person instead of the first person (he didn't say, "I myself had this experience"). This makes some wonder if he is really speaking about himself here, or if he speaks of someone else. But because he transitions into the first person in verse seven, we may be assured that he really writes about himself.

i. Then why does he use the third person at all? Because Paul, in describing this remarkable spiritual experience, is describing just the kind of thing that the "super apostles" among the Corinthian Christians would glory in. When he described his humble experiences in 2 Corinthians 11:23-30, he did not hesitate to write in the first person. No one would think he was glorifying himself as the "super apostles" did. But here, he walks more carefully. Paul does everything he can to relate this experience without bringing glory to himself.

d. **Fourteen years ago**: This dating by Paul does little to help us know when this happened, because scholars are not in agreement regarding when 2 Corinthians was written.

i. Suggestions have been made that the experience he describes happened during Paul's ten years in Syria and Cilicia (Galatians 1:21-2:1), at his stoning in Lystria (Acts 14:19), or during his time in Antioch (Acts 13:1-3).

ii. The important thing to notice is that Paul kept quiet about this for **fourteen years**, and now he mentions it reluctantly.

e. **Whether in the body I do not know, or whether out of the body I do not know, God knows**: Paul doesn't really know if he was **in the body** or **out of the body** during this vision. It seems that in his mind, either one was possible.

i. Many might ask, what really happened to Paul? Was he carried up **in the body** to heaven, or did his spirit separate itself from his body and go there? The whole point of the passage is that if Paul didn't know, we can't know. In fact, Paul emphasizes the point by repeating the idea twice (in verse two and in verse three). Therefore, speculation at this point is useless. "As he could not decide himself, it would be ridiculous in us to attempt it." (Clarke)

f. **Such a one was caught up to the third heaven**: The **third heaven** doesn't suggest different "levels" of heaven (although this is what some ancient Jewish Rabbis believed). Instead, Paul is using terminology common in that day, which referred to the "blue sky" as the *first* heaven, the "starry sky" as the *second* heaven, and the place where God lived and reigned as the *third* heaven.

i. "In the sacred writings *three* heavens only are mentioned. The *first* is the *atmosphere* . . . The *second*, the starry heaven . . . And, *thirdly*, the *place of the blessed*, or the *throne of the Divine glory*." (Clarke)

ii. So, this **one** - whom we understand to be Paul himself - was **caught up to the heaven** where God lives. Paul had a vision or an experience of the throne of God, just as Isaiah (Isaiah 6:1) and John (Revelation 4:1-2) did.

g. **He was caught up into Paradise**: Paul identifies this **third heaven** as **Paradise**. The word **Paradise** is taken from the Persian word for an enclosed, luxurious garden often only found among royalty in the ancient world.

i. Some early Christians wrongly thought **Paradise** was the place where souls of believers went after death to await resurrection. Some of them (like the ancient theologian Origen) even believed **Paradise** was located somewhere on the earth's surface.

h. **And heard inexpressible words, which it is not lawful for a man to utter**: In describing this heavenly vision, Paul doesn't relate anything he *saw*, only a shadowy description of what he **heard**.

i. When we think of this, we realize how different Paul is from most of those who describe their so-called "visions" of heaven today. There is *nothing* self-glorying, self-aggrandizing, or foolish in the description of his experience.

- Paul waited 14 years to say anything about the incident, and when he finally did he said it reluctantly

- He did everything he could in relating the story to take the focus off himself (such as writing in the third person)

- He doesn't bother at all with breathless descriptions of what he actually experienced. Instead, he says nothing of what he saw, and says only that he heard things **not lawful for a man to utter**.

ii. So what did Paul hear? We don't know! They were **inexpressible words, which it is not lawful for a man to utter**. God didn't want us to know, so He didn't give Paul permission to speak.

iii. Nevertheless, some commentators can't resist speculating: "It is probable that the apostle refers to some communication concerning the Divine nature and the Divine economy, of which he was only to make a *general* use in his *preaching* and *writing*. No doubt that what he learned at this time formed the *basis* of all his doctrines." (Clarke)

i. **Of such a one I will boast; yet of myself I will not boast, except in my infirmities**: Paul essentially says that this "nameless" man who had the vision really had something to **boast** about. But "Paul himself" really could only **boast** in his **infirmities**, which was exactly what he did in 2 Corinthians 11:23-30.

i. **Though I might desire to boast, I will not be a fool**: Again, Paul is sharply - and humorously - contrasting himself with the "super apostles" among the Corinthian Christians. They would not hesitate to **boast** about the kind of vision Paul had. In fact, they would write books, make tapes and videos, and go on speaking tours about such a vision! And if they did, each of them would **be a fool**. Paul will not **be a fool**, so he will not boast in this vision.

ii. At the same time, we almost sense that it was important for Paul to communicate to the Corinthian Christians that *he really did have such experiences*. Often, it is easy to think that the only ones who have profound experiences with God are those who **boast** about them constantly. Paul never did boast as the "super apostles" did, but he certainly had profound experiences with God. The proof of those profound experiences was found in his transformed life and powerful, truthful ministry.

iii. Therefore, Paul felt it was important to *mention* this experience but not to *dwell* on it in any way. He wasn't trying to "sell" himself to the Corinthian Christians. In fact, he holds back from his description (**But I forbear**), because he didn't want to persuade the Corinthian Christians that he was just another "super apostle" (**lest anyone should think of me above what he sees me to be or hears from me**). If the Corinthian Christians thought Paul was weak and different from the "super apostles," that was fine with him. He wanted the Corinthian Christians to see the glory of God expressed in weakness, not to see him as "great" as the "super apostles" claimed to be.

j. Why was Paul given this vision? First, he was given it for you and me so that we would benefit from what the Lord showed Paul. Secondly, he was given it because what God told him through this vision sustained him through all the trials of ministry and enabled Paul to give everything God wanted him to give to all generations. This vision helped Paul finish his course.

2. (7) The presence of Paul's thorn in the flesh.

And lest I should be exalted above measure by the abundance of the revelations, a thorn in the flesh was given to me, a messenger of Satan to buffet me, lest I be exalted above measure.

a. **And lest I should be exalted above measure by the abundance of the revelations**: Paul's vision was so impressive that it would have been easy for him to be **exalted above measure by the abundance of the revelations**. He could have gloried in himself or caused others to glory in him because of this experience.

i. Paul was not immune to the danger of pride. No one is. "The best of God's people have in them a root of pride, or a disposition to be *exalted above measure,* upon their receipt of favours from God not common to others." (Poole)

b. **A thorn in the flesh was given to me**: To prevent being **exalted above measure**, Paul was given this. In this, Paul reveals the real reason for telling of his heavenly vision: not to glorify himself but to explain his **thorn in the flesh**.

> i. It seems that everyone could see the **thorn in the flesh** Paul suffered from - it was no secret. His heavenly vision was a secret until now, but everyone saw the **thorn**. Some among the Corinthian Christians probably thought less of Paul because of his **thorn in the flesh**, but they knew nothing of the amazing spiritual experience that lay behind it.

> ii. "He says, 'There was *given* to me.' He reckoned his great trial to be a gift. It is well put. He does not say, 'There was inflicted upon me a thorn in the flesh,' but 'There was given to me.'" (Spurgeon)

c. What is a **thorn in the flesh**? When we think of a **thorn**, we think of a somewhat minor irritation. But the root word Paul used for **thorn** here describes *a tent stake*, not a thumbtack.

> i. In the ancient Greek translation of the Old Testament known as the Septuagint, the word *skolops* (**thorn**) shows "something which frustrates and causes trouble in the lives of those afflicted." (Kruse)

d. **A thorn in the flesh was given to me, a messenger of Satan to buffet me**: In a strange way, the **thorn** was **given** - ultimately given by God - but it was also **a messenger of Satan**.

> i. Satan probably jumped at God's permission to afflict Paul and did so with malice towards the apostle. But God had a purpose in it all and allowed Satan's messenger to successfully keep Paul from being **exalted above measure**.

> ii. **To buffet me** means that this **thorn in the flesh** - the **messenger of Satan** - "punched" Paul. He felt that he was beaten black and blue by this **messenger of Satan**.

> iii. Paul, punched about by the devil? Who would have thought it? "Perhaps you have looked into the face of a Christian who is always smiling, who never seems to have any worry, is always happy and radiant and, as you have thought about your own circumstances, you have said in your heart, 'I wish I were he! He seems to have no problems. He doesn't have to take what I do.' But perhaps you have lived long enough, as I have, to know that sometimes the most radiant face hides great pressures, and often the man who is being most blessed of God is being most buffeted by the devil." (Redpath)

e. It is interesting to consider what a counselor without a Biblical perspective might have said to Paul. Imagine that Paul tells the counselor about his great infirmity, his troublesome "thorn in the flesh," and how Paul feels weak and powerless to continue on against it. We might imagine that the counselor would say, "Well Paul, what you need is a positive mental outlook to meet this problem." Or he might say, "Paul, the power is within you to conquer this infirmity; you should look deep within the inner man to find the resources for success." Perhaps the counselor would then tell Paul, "What you really need a support group of caring individuals." The counselor might suggest Paul take medication for depression. Or he might even seek to challenge Paul by saying, "Paul, if you really had faith, you would be delivered from this thorn in the flesh." Some of this advice might be good in different circumstances, but Paul will take his problem to the Wonderful Counselor, and He has something different to say.

3. (8) Paul's prayer regarding the thorn in the flesh.

Concerning this thing I pleaded with the Lord three times that it might depart from me.

a. **Concerning this thing I pleaded with the Lord**: Paul did exactly what he told others to do in a time of trouble. Paul believed for himself what he wrote in Philippians 4:6: *Be anxious for nothing, but in everything by prayer and supplication, with thanksgiving, let your requests be made known to God.*

b. **I pleaded with the Lord three times**: In fact, Paul *repeatedly* prayed about this thorn in the flesh. We might imagine that when the thorn in the flesh first appeared Paul thought, "This is no problem. I'll just give it to the Lord in prayer." But nothing happened when he prayed. So he thought, "This is a tough one," and prayed again. When nothing happened after praying the third time, he knew God was trying to tell him something.

i. Some think that Paul is using a Hebrew figure of speech that really means much more than **three times**. "That does not mean three times. It is the Hebrew figure for ceaselessly, continuously, over and over again." (Morgan)

ii. Some say it is unspiritual and evidence of little faith to pray for something more than once. That would be surprising to Paul, who **pleaded with the Lord three times**, and to Jesus, who prayed with *the same words* three times in His agony in the Garden of Gethsemane (Mark 14:39-41).

iii. But there was nothing wrong with Paul's prayer. "God respecteth not the arithmetic of our prayers, how many they are; not the rhetoric of our prayers, how neat they are; nor the geometry of our prayers, how long they are; nor the music of our prayers, how melodious they are; nor the logic of our prayers, how methodical they are; but the divinity of our prayers, how heart-sprung they are. Not gifts, but graces prevail in prayer." (Trapp)

c. **Pleaded with the Lord**: Paul's prayer on this matter was *passionate*. We wonder if he wasn't surprised when the prayer was not answered the first or second time.

d. **That it might depart from me**: Paul's initial prayer was to *escape* the suffering this thorn in the flesh brought him. Paul was no masochist. When he suffered, his first instinct was to ask God to take the suffering away.

i. When his passionate and repeated plea was not answered, it must have concerned Paul. It added another dimension to this trial.

- It had a *physical* dimension, in that it was a thorn in the flesh

- It had a *mental* dimension, in that it was a messenger of Satan

- It had a *spiritual* dimension, in that it was an unanswered prayer

e. What exactly was Paul's **thorn in the flesh**? We simply don't have enough information to say precisely, but that hasn't prevented many commentators and teachers from giving their opinion.

i. Some see it mainly as *spiritual harassment*. Others think it was *persecution*. Many suggest that it was a *physical* or *mental* ailment. Some say this was Paul's struggle with lustful and sinful thoughts.

ii. Among Christians, Tertullian gives the earliest recorded guess at the exact nature of Paul's problem. He thought the thorn in the flesh was an earache or a headache.

iii. In more modern times, historian Sir William Ramsay offered the suggestion that Paul's infirmity was a type of malaria common to the area where he served as a missionary. Sufferers of this type of malaria experience attacks when under stress, and they "feel a contempt and loathing for self, and believe that others feel equal contempt and loathing." This malarial fever also produces severe headaches, described by sufferers as being "like a red-hot bar thrust through the forehead."

iv. Each of these suggestions is possible, but God had a definite purpose in not revealing the exact nature of Paul's thorn. If we knew exactly what Paul's thorn was, then everybody who was afflicted - but not in exactly the same way - might doubt that Paul's experience was relevant for them. God wanted everyone with any kind of thorn in the flesh to be able to put themselves in Paul's shoes. "I generally find that each expositor has selected that particular thorn which had pierced his own bosom." (Spurgeon)

4. (9-10) God's provision to Paul through his thorn in the flesh.

And He said to me, "My grace is sufficient for you, for My strength is made perfect in weakness." Therefore most gladly I will rather boast in my infirmities, that the power of Christ may rest upon me. Therefore I take pleasure in infirmities, in reproaches, in needs, in persecutions, in distresses, for Christ's sake. For when I am weak, then I am strong.

a. **And He said to me**: God had a response for Paul. The answer was not what Paul initially hoped for or expected, but God still had a response for Paul. We often close our ears to God if He responds in a way we did not hope for or expect.

b. **My grace is sufficient for you, for My strength is made perfect in weakness**: Instead of removing the thorn from Paul's life, God gave and would keep giving His **grace** to Paul. The **grace** God gave Paul was **sufficient** to meet his every need.

i. Paul was desperate in his desire to find relief from this burden, but there are two ways of relief. It can come by *removing* the load or by *strengthening* the shoulder that bears the load. Instead of taking away the thorn, God strengthened Paul under it, and God would show His strength through Paul's apparent **weakness**.

ii. To do this, Paul had to believe that God's **grace is sufficient**. We really don't believe God's grace is sufficient until we believe we are *insufficient*. For many of us, especially in American culture, this is a huge obstacle. We are the people who idolize the "self-made man" and want to rely on ourselves. But we can't receive God's strength until we know our weakness. We can't receive the sufficiency of God's grace until we know our own insufficiency.

iii. "Great tribulation brings out the great strength of God. If you never feel inward conflicts and sinking of soul, you do not know much of the upholding power of God; but if you go down, down, into the depths of soul-anguish till the deep threatens to shut her mouth upon you, and then the Lord rides upon a cherub and does fly, yea, rides upon the wings of the wind and delivers your soul, and catches you away to the third heaven of delight, then you perceive the majesty of divine grace. Oh, there must be the weakness of man, felt, recognized, and mourned over, or else the strength of the Son of God will never be perfected in us." (Spurgeon)

c. **My grace is sufficient**: How did God's **grace** make the difference? How did it meet Paul's need at this point?

i. **Grace** *could meet Paul's need because it expresses God's acceptance and plea-sure in us.* When we receive His grace, we enjoy our status of favor and approval in God's eyes. Grace means that God likes us, that He is favorably disposed towards us and that we have His approval and promise of care.

ii. **Grace** *could meet Paul's need because it was available all the time.* When we sin or fail, it does not put us outside the reach of God's grace. Since grace is given freely to us in Jesus, it can't be taken away later because we stumble or fall. When we come to God by faith through the blood of Jesus, His grace is ever ready to meet us and to minister to our insufficiencies.

iii. **Grace** *could meet Paul's need because it was the very strength of God.* So much of the power of this world is expressed in things that can only bring harm and destruction, but God loves to show His power through His goodness and grace. Sometimes we associate goodness with cow-ardice or timidity. When we do, we take a worldly perspective about power and strength, and we deny God's truth about the strength of grace and love. Grace is not weak or wimpy. Instead, it is the power of God to fulfill what we lack.

d. **My grace is sufficient for you**: You may emphasize any aspect of this you please.

i. "My **grace** is sufficient for you." Grace is the favor and love of God in action. It means He loves us and is pleased by us. Can you hear it from God? "My love is enough for you." Isn't it true?

ii. "**My** grace is sufficient for you." Whose grace is it? It is the grace of Jesus. Isn't His love, His favor, enough? What will Jesus fail at? Re-member too that Jesus suffered thorns, so He cares and He knows.

iii. "My grace **is** sufficient for you." It **is** right now. Not that it will be some day, but right now, at this moment, His grace is sufficient. You thought something had to change before His grace would be enough. You thought, "His grace *was* sufficient once, His grace *may be* suffi-cient again, but not now, not with what I am going through." Despite that feeling, God's word stands. "My grace **is** sufficient for you." Spurgeon wrote, "It is easy to believe in grace for the past and the future, but to rest in it for the immediate necessity is true faith. Be-liever, it is *now* that grace is sufficient: even at this moment it *is* enough for thee."

iv. "My grace is **sufficient** for you." Redpath explains this aspect best: "Do you see the humor of the situation? God's grace: me. His grace sufficient for little me! How absurd to think that it could ever be any different! As if a little fish could swim in the ocean and fear lest it might drink it dry! The grace of our crucified, risen, exalted, triumphant Saviour, the Lord of all glory, is surely sufficient for me! Do you not think it is rather modest of the Lord to say *sufficient?*"

v. "My grace is sufficient **for you.**" I'm so glad God didn't say, "My grace is sufficient for Paul the Apostle." I might have felt left out. But God made it broad enough. **You** can be the "**you**" in **for you.** God's grace is sufficient **for you!** Are you beyond it? Are you so different? Is your thorn worse than Paul's or worse than many others who have known the triumph of Jesus? Of course not. This sufficient grace is **for you.**

vi. "This sufficiency is declared without any limiting words, and therefore I understand the passage to mean that the grace of our Lord Jesus is sufficient to uphold thee, sufficient to strengthen thee, sufficient to comfort thee, sufficient to make thy trouble useful to thee, sufficient to enable thee to triumph over it, sufficient to bring thee out of it, sufficient to bring thee out of ten thousand like it, sufficient to bring thee home to heaven . . . O child of God, I wish it were possible to put into words this all-sufficiency, but it is not. Let me retract my speech: I am glad that it cannot be put into words, for if so it would be finite, but since we never can express it, glory be to God it is inexhaustible, and our demands upon it can never be too great. Here let me press upon you the pleasing duty of taking home the promise personally at this moment, for no believer here need be under any fear, since for him also, at this very instant, the grace of the Lord Jesus is sufficient." (Spurgeon)

vii. "John Bunyan has the following passage, which exactly expresses what I myself have experienced. He says that he was full of sadness and terror, but suddenly these words broke in upon him with great power, and three times together the words sounded in his ears, "My grace is sufficient for thee; my grace is sufficient for thee; my grace is sufficient for thee." And "Oh! Bethought," says he, "that every word was a mighty word unto me; as '*My*,' and '*grace*,' and '*sufficient*,' and '*for thee*'; they were then, and sometimes are still, far bigger than others be." He who knows, like the bee, how to suck honey from flowers, may well linger over each one of these words and drink in unutterable content." (Spurgeon)

e. **Therefore most gladly I will rather boast in my infirmities, that the power of Christ may rest upon me:** Through his **infirmities,** God made Paul completely dependent on His **grace** and on His **strength,** but it was all for good. Paul's continued - even forced - dependence upon God made him stronger than he would have ever been if his revelations had made him proud and self-sufficient.

i. Many of us think that real Christian maturity is when we come to a place where we are somewhat "independent" of God. The idea is that we have our act so together that we don't need to rely on God so much day to day, moment to moment. This isn't Christian maturity at all. God deliberately engineered debilitating circumstances into Paul's life so he would be in constant, total dependence on God's grace and God's strength.

ii. Many people see God as a parent that we outgrow. Once we're mature and once we have overcome certain obstacles in life, we can shake off God just the same as we shook off the authority of our parents. In this pattern, some of us treat God the same way we treat our parents. We give Him a measure of respect, we give Him His due - but we no longer feel we really have to *obey* Him any more. In our hearts, we have moved out of the house. We think we can make our own rules in life as long as we have supper at God's house once a week and give the Him a little recognition.

iii. Many harbor a longing for the day when the Christian life will become "easy." We hope for a time when the major struggles with sin are behind us, and now we go on to bigger and better things without much of a struggle. That day is an illusion. If the Apostle Paul himself constantly experienced weakness, who are we to think that we will surpass him?

iv. In fact, the *illusion* of strength and independence actually leaves someone in a weaker place. "There is nothing more hindering to the work of God than the uplifted and proud Christian." (Morgan)

v. "Ministers of the Gospel especially should banish all thoughts of their own cleverness, intellectual ability, culture, sufficiency for their work, and learn that only when they are emptied can they be filled, and only when they know themselves to be nothing are they ready for God to work through them." (Maclaren)

vi. "God works through the man who has been wiped clean and turned inside out, his life emptied before the Lord until he is hopelessly weak, that no flesh might glory in His presence." (Redpath)

f. **Therefore I take pleasure in infirmities**: In the end, Paul does not resign himself to his fate; he welcomes it. He rejoices that God has forced him to rely on the grace and strength of God all the more so he can say, **"when I am weak, then I am strong."**

i. Paul was at such a level of spiritual strength and maturity that God had to deliberately introduce a *thorn in the flesh*. Most of us provide our own thorns, and an honest look shows us enough weakness to make us constantly and totally rely on the grace and strength of Jesus. Yet even if we were to grow to the spiritual strength and maturity of a Paul, God would say to us as well: "I need to keep you depending on Me in everything. Here is something to depend on Me for." This is a place of *victory*, not of *discouragement*.

ii. "In the Christian perspective there is no place for the aimless non-resistance of dispirited resignation." (Hughes)

g. Paul's **pleasure in infirmities** is not the sick musing of an ascetic, thinking that we are justified before God by our sufferings. Paul didn't *seek* his thorn in the flesh, it came to him.

i. "The concept, so pernicious in the Church at a later date, of courting martyrdom, of practising asceticism, and even of embracing dirt, disease, and destitution as means to the acquisition of favour before God, is diametrically opposed to the Apostle's mind and to the whole tenor of the gospel in the New Testament, for it is a concept governing a way of life *for one's own sake*, with a view to making oneself righteous and acceptable before God - a concept of works, not faith." (Hughes)

h. **For when I am weak, then I am strong**: What triumph! What can the world do to such a man so firm in the grip of Jesus? God did not allow this *thorn in the flesh* to punish Paul or to keep him weak for the sake of weakness. God allowed it to show a divine strength in Paul.

i. Think about this man Paul. Was he a weak or strong man? The man who traveled the ancient world spreading the gospel of Jesus despite the fiercest persecutions, who endured shipwrecks and imprisonment, who preached to kings and slaves, who established strong churches and trained up their leaders was not a weak man. In light of his life and accomplishments, we would say that Paul was a very strong man. But he was only strong because he knew his weaknesses and looked outside himself for the strength of God's grace. If we want lives of such strength, we also must understand and admit our weakness and look to God alone for the grace that will strengthen us for any task. It was the grace-filled Paul who said, "*I can do all things through Christ who strengthens me.*" (Philippians 4:13)

ii. "The valleys are watered with rain to make them fruitful while the summits of lofty mountains remain dry. A man must become a valley

if he wants to receive the heavenly rain of God's spiritual grace."
(Calvin)

iii. "From all this I gather, that the worst trial a man may have may be
the best possession he has in this world; that the messenger of Satan
may be as good to him as his guardian angel; that it may be as well for
him to be buffeted of Satan as ever it was to be caressed of the Lord
himself; that it may be essential to our soul's salvation that we should
do business not only on deep waters, but on waters that cast up mire
and dirt. The worst form of trial may, nevertheless, be our best present
portion." (Spurgeon)

i. To summarize, instead of using his experience to glorify himself (as the
"super apostles" among the Corinthian Christians did), Paul relates how
his whole glorious experience humbled him more than ever.

i. All Paul's enemies could see was the thorn; they could not see how
and why it was there. But Paul knew, so he rejoiced even in his thorn
in the flesh.

ii. Of course, the greatest example of the principle Paul communi-
cates here was lived by Jesus Himself. "Could anyone on earth be
more meek than the Son of God to be hung on the cross, hung in our
place that He might redeem us from our sins? As that point of absolute weakness was met by the mighty power of God as He raised Him
from the dead, I wonder if the pressure of the thorn in Paul's life was
a reminder of the power of the cross." (Redpath)

iii. Yet, we should never think that in our lives, the mere presence of a
thorn means the glory and strength of Jesus would shine in us and
through us. You can resist God's grace and refuse to set your mind on
Jesus, and then find your thorn cursing you instead of blessing you.
"Without the sanctifying power of the Holy Spirit, thorns are pro-
ductive of evil rather than good. In many people, their thorn in the
flesh does not appear to have fulfilled any admirable design at all; it
has created another vice, instead of removing a temptation."
(Spurgeon)

5. (11-13) Conclusion to Paul's "foolish boasting."

**I have become a fool in boasting; you have compelled me. For I ought
to have been commended by you; for in nothing was I behind the most
eminent apostles, though I am nothing. Truly the signs of an apostle
were accomplished among you with all perseverance, in signs and wonders and mighty deeds. For what is it in which you were inferior to
other churches, except that I myself was not burdensome to you? Forgive me this wrong!**

a. **I have become a fool in boasting**: Since he began this section in 2 Corinthians 10:1, Paul was forced to boast more than he wanted to before the Corinthian Christians. Paul is almost apologizing for writing so much about himself, because he would much rather write about Jesus.

b. **For I ought to have been commended by you; for in nothing was I behind the most eminent apostles, though I am nothing**: If Paul thought his "boasting" was foolish, why did he do it at all? Not for his sake, but for the sake of the Corinthian Christians. They did not defend Paul's character and standing as an apostle before the **most eminent apostles** who criticized and undermined Paul.

> i. It wasn't so much that the *presence* of the **most eminent apostles** bothered Paul. It was their *influence* among the Corinthian Christians that bothered the true apostle.

c. **Truly the signs of an apostle were accomplished among you . . . in signs and wonders and mighty deeds**: Paul could also point to the **signs and wonders and mighty deeds** that **were accomplished** among the Corinthian Christians. Each of these was evidence of Paul's apostolic standing.

d. **For what is it in which you were inferior to other churches**: If Paul is inferior in any way, it is only in that he refused to take money from the Corinthian Christians. So, he sarcastically asks their forgiveness: **Forgive me this wrong!**

> i. "A pleasant irony, such as whereof this Epistle is full." (Trapp)
>
> ii. "It is the *privilege* of the Churches of Christ to support the ministry of his Gospel among them. Those who do not contribute their part to the support of the gospel ministry either care nothing for it, or derive no good from it." (Clarke)

B. Paul announces his third trip to Corinth.

1. (14-18) Paul isn't trying to deceive the Corinthians.

Now *for* the third time I am ready to come to you. And I will not be burdensome to you; for I do not seek yours, but you. For the children ought not to lay up for the parents, but the parents for the children. And I will very gladly spend and be spent for your souls; though the more abundantly I love you, the less I am loved. But be that *as it may*, I did not burden you. Nevertheless, being crafty, I caught you by cunning! Did I take advantage of you by any of those whom I sent to you? I urged Titus, and sent our brother with *him*. Did Titus take advantage of you? Did we not walk in the same spirit? Did *we* not *walk* in the same steps?

a. **Now for the third time I am ready to come to you**: On his first visit to Corinth, Paul founded the church and stayed *a year and six months* (Acts 18:11). His second visit was a brief, painful visit in between the writing of 1 Corinthians and 2 Corinthians. Now he is prepared to come for a **third time**.

b. **And I will not be burdensome to you**: Paul lets the Corinthian Christians know that when he comes, though he will receive a collection for the saints in Judea (2 Corinthians 8), he will not receive money from them for his personal support. He will continue his previous practice among the Corinthian Christians of supporting himself and he **will not be burdensome** to the Corinthian Christians.

> i. A minister may be **burdensome** to a congregation by receiving support when it is not appropriate or by receiving too much support. "He who labours for the cause of God should be supported by the cause of God; but woe to that man who aggrandizes himself and grows *rich* by the *spoils of the faithful!* And to him especially who has made a fortune out of the *pence* of the poor! In such a man's heart the *love of money* must have its *throne*. As to his professed *spirituality*, it is *nothing*; he is a *whited sepulchre*, and an abomination in the sight of the Lord." (Clarke)

c. **For I do not seek yours, but you**: This is the testimony of every godly minister. They do not serve for what they can get *from* God's people but for what they can give *to* God's people. They are shepherds, not hirelings.

> i. This is the heart of Jesus towards us. We often think that what God really wants is what we *have*; but He really wants *us*. Jesus selflessly seeks our good, and His heart is *for* us, not for what He can "get" *from* us.

> ii. "Paul is only a faint shadow of the Lord Jesus; and if these qualities are found in his life, it is only because they were found completely in the life of Jesus Christ our Lord." (Redpath)

d. **For the children ought not to lay up for the parents, but the parents for the children**: This explains part of the reason why Paul did not want to receive support from the Corinthian Christians. Since he was their spiritual "father" and they were his spiritual "children," it made sense that they should not feel "burdened" to support him.

> i. At the same time, this is not a compliment towards the Corinthian Christians. Since Paul did gratefully receive support from other churches (Philippians 4:10-19), we know this was not his policy towards all churches. Instead, it is as if Paul is saying, "You Corinthian Christians are not mature enough to support me yet. You are still

spiritual children. When you grow up some, you can be partners with me in the work and support me. But until then I am glad to support myself."

e. **I will very gladly spend and be spent for your souls**: Paul did not resent the lack of support from the Corinthian Christians. Certainly, he would have appreciated it, but more for what it *said about them* than for what it *did for him*. For himself, Paul was glad to give; he would **very gladly spend and be spent for your souls**.

i. Paul had this heart, even though the Corinthian Christians were unappreciative. In fact, Paul puts it painfully: **the more abundantly I love you, the less I am loved**. There is hurt in those words! Yet, Paul did not allow that hurt to cripple him or even to rob his joy in serving and living. He would still **very gladly spend and be spent for** the Corinthian Christians.

ii. We can give and do it in any number of ways; but do we resent it when we give or serve? A good way to measure this is to see our reaction when our service is unappreciated. Do we resent it? Paul's service was unappreciated by the Corinthian Christians, yet he did not resent it. Instead, he would **very gladly spend and be spent for your souls**.

f. **Nevertheless, being crafty, I caught you with guile!** Here is Paul being sarcastic again. Some among the Corinthian Christians accused Paul of **being crafty**. Their accusation probably went like this: "Sure Paul won't take any support money from you, but he will trick you by taking the collection that is supposed to be for the Jerusalem Christians and then put it in his own pocket." In response Paul sarcastically said, "You bet I'm **being crafty**! I've **caught you with guile** and tricked you superbly!"

i. Paul's opponents, the *most eminent apostles* mentioned in 2 Corinthians 11:5 and 12:11, were in ministry at least partly for the money. They could not bear the fact that Paul didn't care about money in the ministry, so they assigned *their* motives *to him*.

ii. Some have thought that Paul spoke seriously here and admitted that he was **crafty** and used **guile** in his ministry to the Corinthian Christians. "Many persons suppose that the words, *being crafty, I caught you with guile*, are the words of the apostle, and not of his slanderers; and therefore have concluded that it is lawful to use guile, deceit, [and so forth], in order to serve a good and religious purpose. This doctrine is abominable; and the words are most evidently those of the apostle's detractors, against which he defends his conduct in the two following verses." (Clarke)

g. **Did I take advantage of you?** Paul proves that the charge he is **being crafty** is false. He reminds the Corinthian Christians that neither Paul nor any of his associates had ever behaved in a financially inappropriate way before the Corinthians.

2. (19-21) Paul encourages the Corinthians to repent before he comes.

Again, do you think that we excuse ourselves to you? We speak before God in Christ. But *we do* all things, beloved, for your edification. For I fear lest, when I come, I shall not find you such as I wish, and *that* I shall be found by you such as you do not wish; lest *there be* contentions, jealousies, outbursts of wrath, selfish ambitions, backbitings, whisperings, conceits, tumults; lest, when I come again, my God will humble me among you, and I shall mourn for many who have sinned before and have not repented of the uncleanness, fornication, and lewdness which they have practiced.

a. **Again, do you think that we excuse ourselves to you? We speak before God in Christ.** Paul is concerned that his defense before the Corinthians Christians may be taken as just excuse making. But Paul is not making excuses; he has nothing to excuse. Instead he boldly says, "**We speak before God in Christ.**" Paul proclaimed the truth before God, not excusing himself before the Corinthian Christians.

b. **We do all things, beloved, for your edification:** *Everything* Paul did for the Corinthian Christians he did to build them up in the Lord. Every letter he wrote, every visit he made, every prayer he prayed was with one goal: to build up the Corinthian Christians in Jesus Christ. His heart was for *them*, not for *himself.*

i. If Paul's opponents - the *most eminent apostles* mentioned in 2 Corinthians 11:5 and 12:11 - were to speak honestly, they would say: "We do all things, beloved, for *our* edification." But Paul was a different kind of man.

ii. "It is not his purpose to make the Corinthians squirm, but to bring them to their senses, to help them to rid themselves of the narcotic effect produced on them by the false apostles who had invaded their community." (Hughes)

c. **For I fear lest, when I come, I shall not find you such as I wish:** Paul is worried that he will find the same old problems among the Corinthian Christians when he visits a third time and that they would still be unrepentant.

i. Just so they know exactly what Paul is writing about, he makes it clear: **lest there be contentions, jealousies, outbursts of wrath,**

selfish ambitions, backbitings, whisperings, conceits, tumults. All these were the fruit of the worldly thinking the Corinthian Christians bought into, and these must change before Paul comes for his third visit to Corinth.

d. **I shall be found by you such as you do not wish**: Looking forward to his next visit, Paul warns the Corinthian Christians. If they are not in a state pleasing to Paul (before the Lord), then they will find *him* to be in a state not pleasing to them.

e. **Lest, when I come again, my God will humble me among you**: If the Corinthian Christians were still stuck in their worldly thinking, Paul would be *humbled* among them. He would have reason to think, "I must not be a very good apostle or leader because these Corinthian Christians will not respond to me." That was not the whole truth, but it would still **humble** Paul.

i. **And I shall mourn for many**: If the Corinthian Christians were mired in their worldliness when Paul came the third time, he would be angry, and he would be firm. But he would also be *humbled*, and he would also **mourn**. As much as anything, the worldliness of the Corinthian Christians grieved Paul and made him **mourn for many**.

ii. "Paul reveals to us the mind of a true and sincere pastor when he says that he will look on the sins of others with grief." (Calvin)

f. **Who have sinned before and have not repented of the uncleanness, fornication, and lewdness which they have practiced**: Paul's anger and mourning would not be directed to those who had sinned. More specifically, it would be directed to those **who have sinned before and have not repented**. Paul did not ask for perfection; he only asked for repentance.

2 Corinthians 13 - Examine Yourselves

A. Paul warns the Corinthians to examine themselves before he comes.

1. (1-4) Paul promises to come with severity, if necessary.

This *will be* the third *time* I am coming to you. "By the mouth of two or three witnesses every word shall be established." I have told you before, and foretell as if I were present the second time, and now being absent I write to those who have sinned before, and to all the rest, that if I come again I will not spare; since you seek a proof of Christ speaking in me, who is not weak toward you, but mighty in you. For though He was crucified in weakness, yet He lives by the power of God. For we also are weak in Him, but we shall live with Him by the power of God toward you.

a. **This will be the third time I am coming to you**: On his first visit to Corinth, Paul founded the church and stayed *a year and six months* (Acts 18:11). His second visit was a brief, painful visit in between the writing of 1 Corinthians and 2 Corinthians. Now he is prepared to come for a **third time**.

b. **By the mouth of two or three witnesses every word shall be established**: Paul quotes this passage from Deuteronomy 19:15, and quotes it in reference to his coming visit. Either the **two or three witnesses** are Paul's three visits or they are the testimony of his associates. The point of the quotation is to remind the Corinthian Christians that he comes this time as a judge, not an investigator. He has enough evidence to write, "**If I come again I will not spare.**"

i. Those are strong words: **I will not spare**. However, the situation among the Corinthian Christians called for strong leadership. A Christian pastor must never let authority corrupt into authoritarianism, yet, "Rebellion against an appointed minister is rebellion against the higher power that appointed him." (Hughes)

c. **Since you see a proof of Christ speaking in me**: Paul's opponents, the *most eminent apostles* among the Corinthian Christians (2 Corinthians 11:5 and 12:11), said they wanted to see more "power" from Paul. He seemed too weak and humble for their liking. So Paul addressed this thinking: "You want to see **proof of Christ speaking in me**? Fine. When I come the third time, you will see **the power of God** in my rebuke as I clean house. So clean it up before I come."

> i. **For though He was crucified in weakness, yet He lives by the power of God. For we also are weak in Him, but we shall live with Him by the power of God toward you.** Just as Jesus displayed weakness yet now reigns in power, so Paul will come with similar power after showing the Corinthian Christians his weakness.

> ii. "It would seem that in their immaturity the Corinthians were unimpressed by Christlike gentleness and meekness . . . but were overawed by arbitrary displays of power." (Harris)

2. (5-10) A plea for self examination.

Examine yourselves *as to* whether you are in the faith. Test yourselves. Do you not know yourselves, that Jesus Christ is in you?; unless indeed you are disqualified. But I trust that you will know that we are not disqualified. Now I pray to God that you do no evil, not that we should appear approved, but that you should do what is honorable, though we may seem disqualified. For we can do nothing against the truth, but for the truth. For we are glad when we are weak and you are strong. And this also we pray, that you may be made complete. Therefore I write these things being absent, lest being present I should use sharpness, according to the authority which the Lord has given me for edification and not for destruction.

a. **Examine yourselves as to whether you are in the faith. Test yourselves. Do you not know yourselves, that Jesus Christ is in you?** Paul asks the Corinthian Christians to consider a sobering question: "Am I really a Christian?"

> i. We are rightly concerned that every believer has the assurance of salvation and knows how to endure the attacks that come in this area from Satan. At the same time we also understand that there are some who *assume* or *presume* they are Christians when they are not. It is a challenge to all: **Examine yourselves as to whether you are in the faith. Test yourselves. Do you not know yourselves, that Jesus Christ is in you?**

> ii. We are often very ready to examine and test others, but first - and always first - we must examine and test ourselves. "That was the trouble

at Corinth. They criticized Paul and failed to examine themselves."
(Redpath)

iii. "To examine yourself, in fact, is to submit to the examination and
scrutiny of Jesus Christ the Lord - and this never to fix attention on
sin but on Christ - and to ask Him to reveal that in you which grieves
His Spirit; to ask Him to give you grace that it might be put away and
cleansed in His precious blood." Self examination "takes the chill away
from your soul, it takes the hardness away from your heart, it takes the
shadows away from your life, it sets the prisoner free." (Redpath)

iv. "Now, 'prove yourselves.' Do not merely sit in your closet and look
at yourselves alone, but go out into this busy world and see what kind
of piety you have. Remember, many a man's religion will stand examination that will not stand proof. We may sit at home and look at our
religion, and say, 'Well, I think this will do!' " (Spurgeon)

v. **Unless indeed you are disqualified**: Paul knew there were some
among the Corinthian Christians who were **disqualified** for eternal
life and salvation. Their thinking was worldly because they were of
the world, not of the Lord. This is a hard truth to confront, but it is
better to know *now* than when it is too late. The word for **disqualified** is simply the negative of the word for **test** in this same passage.
If we don't **examine** ourselves and **test** ourselves now, we may find
that we ultimately don't pass the **test** and are **disqualified**.

b. **Do you not know yourselves, that Jesus Christ is in you?** What are
we to look for when we **examine** and **test** ourselves? We are to see if
Jesus Christ is in you. We are not to look for perfection - in ourselves or
in others - but we should see real evidence of Jesus Christ in us.

i. "Now, what is it to have Jesus Christ in you? The true Christian
carries the cross in his heart; and a cross inside the heart, my friends,
is one of the sweetest cures for a cross on the back. If you have a
cross in your heart - Christ crucified in you, the hope of glory - all the
crosses of this world's troubles will seem to you light enough, and you
will easily be able to sustain it. Christ in the heart means Christ believed in, Christ beloved, Christ trusted, Christ espoused, Christ com-
muned with, Christ as our daily food, and ourselves as the temple and
palace wherein Jesus Christ daily walks." (Spurgeon)

c. **But I trust that you will know that we are not disqualified**: Paul
anticipates a counter-question. "Paul, you ask us to examine ourselves.
Well, why don't you examine yourself? Maybe you aren't a Christian after
all!" Paul dismisses this question out of hand. It is so apparent that **we are
not disqualified** that he simply trusts that they recognize the truth of it.

i. Even so, Paul admitted, **though we may seem to be disqualified.** If one judges a genuine Christian life by worldly standards (emphasizing "power" and "success"), Paul might **seem to be disqualified.** It was by these standards that Job's friends were convinced that his hardships were the result of sin in his life. However, one could say that only by judging with worldly standards.

d. **For we can do nothing against the truth**: Paul, even as an apostle, could **do nothing against the truth.** Even the apostles were not above the truth. Paul could only work effectively **for the truth**, not **against the truth.**

i. "This passage is of special interest as fixing the limits of all ecclesiastical power, whether ordinary or miraculous . . . The promise of our Lord, that what the church binds on earth shall be bound in heaven, is limited by the condition that her decisions be in accordance with the truth." (Hodge)

e. **For we are glad when we are weak and you are strong**: If Paul's weakness could contribute to the strength of the Corinthian Christians, he would be **glad.** His real concern was that the Corinthians **may be made complete.**

i. To **be made complete** is basically the same idea as in 2 Corinthians 12:19: *we do all things, beloved, for your edification.* Paul wanted to build up the Corinthian Christians, to make them **complete.** They were already a body strong in spiritual gifts and personal testimony (1 Corinthians 1:4-7), but their strength was not complete. They were not like a building that was just a foundation and a bit of rubble. They were like a building built tall and strong - for one and a half walls, with the other walls crumbling or barely started. Paul wanted them to be **made complete.**

f. **Therefore I write these things being absent, lest being present I should use sharpness**: Paul preferred that the Corinthian Christians would clean up their act *before* he came to see them. He wanted to use his **authority** for **edification**, not **destruction.**

B. Conclusion to the letter.

1. (11) Concluding exhortation.

Finally, brethren, farewell. Become complete. Be of good comfort, be of one mind, live in peace; and the God of love and peace will be with you.

a. **Finally, brethren, farewell**: **Farewell** is much better translated *rejoice.* Even though Paul has been severe with the Corinthian Christians, all was written to the end that they would enjoy the joy of walking in a right relationship with God.

b. **Become complete**: In 2 Corinthians 13:9, Paul revealed that he prayed that *you may be made complete*. Now he exhorts them to help answer his prayer as he challenges them to **become complete**.

> i. As Christians, we shouldn't excuse and neglect areas of our life by saying, "I'm just not into that" or "That's just my weak point." We certainly cannot work on everything at once before the Lord, but we can have a heart to **become complete**.

c. **Be of good comfort, be of one mind, live in peace**: By exhorting the Corinthian Christians to do these things, Paul proves an important point. These are at least partially in our power to do. We often think that our **comfort**, or being **of one mind**, and our being at **peace** with others just depends on *them*. In part that is true, but it also depends on *us*. We need to let God worry about their part, and we can worry about our part.

> i. It costs something to work hard to **be of good comfort, be of one mind,** and to **live in peace**; but the reward is worth it: **the God of love and peace will be with you.** If you feel that God isn't with you, perhaps it is because you are resisting and rejecting His call to **be of good comfort, be of one mind,** and to **live in peace**.

2. (12-14) Final words.

Greet one another with a holy kiss. All the saints greet you. The grace of the Lord Jesus Christ, and the love of God, and the communion of the Holy Spirit *be* with you all. Amen.

a. **Greet one another with a holy kiss**: The idea of greeting **one another with a holy kiss** was common in that ancient culture. Our cultural equivalent is a handshake or a hug and a warm greeting.

> i. The fact that it is a **holy** kiss shows that it had nothing to do with romantic affection. It was commonly practiced as a warm greeting in the early church but was rarely done on Good Friday, in remembrance of Judas' kiss that betrayed Jesus. In later times, the practice was thought inappropriate. In 1250, in England, the Archbishop of York introduced a "peace-board," which was first kissed by the clergy and then passed around to the congregation.

> ii. "The fact that the kiss was described as *holy* indicates that erotic overtones were excluded, the kiss was a greeting, a sign of peace and Christian *agape*." (Morgan)

> iii. Hodge wisely relates the practice to our modern culture: "It is not a command of perpetual obligation, as the spirit of the command is

that Christians should express their mutual love in the way sanctioned by the age and community in which they live."

b. **The grace of the Lord Jesus Christ, and the love of God, and the communion of the Holy Spirit be with you all.** This is the only place in the New Testament where the Father, the Son, and the Holy Spirit are mentioned together in this kind of blessing. Paul wanted the Corinthian Christians to be completely blessed by everything God is.

i. In essence, Paul wanted them to be blessed as true *Christians*. "For a Christian is one who seeks and enjoys the grace of the Lord Jesus, the love of God, and the communion of the Holy Ghost." (Hodge)

Second Corinthians - Bibliography

This is a bibliography of books cited in the commentary. Of course, there are many other worthy books on 2 Corinthians, but these are listed for the benefit of readers who wish to check sources.

Alford, Henry *The New Testament for English Readers, Volume II, Part I* (London: Rivingtons, 1869)

Barclay, William *The Letters to the Corinthians* (Philadelphia: Westminster Press, 1975)

Bernard, J.H. "The Second Epistle to the Corinthians," *The Expositor's Greek Testament, Volume III* (London: Hodder and Stoughton)

Calvin, John *The Second Epistle of Paul the Apostle to the Corinthians and the Epistles to Timothy, Titus and Philemon*, translated by T.A. Smail (Grand Rapids, Michigan: Eerdmans, 1964)

Clarke, Adam *The New Testament with a Commentary and Critical Notes, Volume II* (New York: Eaton & Mains, 1831)

Harris, Murray J. "2 Corinthians," *The Expositor's Bible Commentary, Volume 10: Romans - Galatians* (Grand Rapids, Michigan: Zondervan, 1976)

Hodge, Charles *I & II Corinthians* (Edinburgh: Banner of Truth Trust, 1988, reprint of 1857 edition)

Hughes, Philip E. *The Second Epistle to the Corinthians* (Grand Rapids, Michigan: Eerdmans, 1962)

Kruse, Colin *2 Corinthians* (Grand Rapids, Michigan: Eerdmans/IVP, 1987)

Maclaren, Alexander *Expostions of Holy Scripture, Volume Fourteen* (Grand Rapids, Michigan: Baker, 1984)

Morgan, G. Campbell *An Exposition of the Whole Bible* (Old Tappan, New Jersey: Revell, 1959)

Morgan, G. Campbell *The Corinthian Letters of Paul* (Old Tappan, New Jersey: Revell, 1946)

Poole, Matthew *A Commentary on the Holy Bible, Volume III: Matthew-Revelation* (London: Banner of Truth Trust, 1969, first published in 1685)

Redpath, Alan *Blessings Out of Buffetings – Studies in Second Corinthians* (Grand Rapids, Michigan: Revell, 1993)

Robertson, Archibald T. *Word Pictures in the New Testament, Volume IV* (Nashville: Broadman Press, 1933)

Smith, Chuck *New Testament Study Guide* (Costa Mesa, California: The Word for Today, 1982)

Spurgeon, Charles Haddon *The New Park Street Pulpit, Volumes 1-6* and *The Metropolitan Tabernacle Pulpit, Volumes 7-63* (Pasadena, Texas: Pilgrim Publications, 1990)

Trapp, John *A Commentary on the Old and New Testaments, Volume Five* (Eureka, California: Tanski Publications, 1997)

Vincent, Marvin R. *Vincent's Word Studies of the New Testament, Volume III* (McLean, Virginia: MacDonald)

Wiersbe, Warren W. *Be Wise* (Wheaton, Illinios: Victor Books, 1989)

Much thanks to the many who helped prepare this commentary. My wife, Inga-Lill, and our children give so much support in this and all the ministry. This is the first time working with the talented Marianne van de Vrede for proofreading and editorial help. Marianne deserves great thanks and my warmest regards for both rescuing this book and helping me with writing skills. Craig Brewer created the cover and helped with the layout. Kara Valeri helped with graphic design. Gayle Erwin provided both inspiration and practical guidance. I am often amazed at the remarkable kindness of others, and thanks to all who give the gift of encouragement. With each year that passes, faithful friends and supporters become all the more precious. Through you all, God has been better to me than I have ever deserved.

David Guzik is the Pastor of Calvary Chapel of Simi Valley. David and his wife, Inga-Lill, live in Simi Valley with their children, Aan-Sofie, Nathan, and Jonathan. You can e-mail David at davidguzik@calvarychapel.com

For more resources by David Guzik, go to www.enduringword.com

More Bible Study Resources from Enduring Word Media

Ask for these works from your local Christian bookstore, or order directly from Enduring Word Media.

Books - Bible Commentary

Genesis (ISBN: 1-56599-049-8)

Acts (ISBN: 1-56599-047-1)

First Corinthians (ISBN: 1-56599-045-5)

Revelation (ISBN: 1-56599-043-9)

Software

New Testament & More (ISBN: 1-56599-048-X)

This CD-ROM gives immediate access to thousands of pages of verse-by-verse Bible commentary through all of the New Testament and many Old Testament books. For ease of use, commentary is available in both Acrobat and HTML format. Also includes bonus audio resources - hours of David Guzik's teaching in mp3 format

Audio Resources

David Guzik's teaching is available on cassette tape and on mp3 cd-rom. Contact Enduring Word Media for a catalog.

Enduring Word Media

www.enduringword.com
ewm@enduringword.com
23 West Easy Street, #204
Simi Valley, CA 93065
(805) 582-6545

LaVergne, TN USA
25 March 2011
221633LV00006B/115/A